Cookie

More than a Cinderella Story —
no one would have dreamed that a drug-addicted prostitute
working the seamiest byways of New York
could be so completely transformed.

THE AUTOBIOGRAPHY OF
COOKIE RODRIGUEZ
WITH NANCY ANDERSON

ACCLAIMED BOOKS

Acclaimed Books
Box 18186
Dallas, Texas 75218

Copyright © 1983 by Acclaimed Books
First Edition

ISBN 0-932294-04-9
Library of Congress Catalog Card Number: 80-6987-3

Printed in the United States of America

Scripture quotations are taken from the *King James Version*.

Distributed by Acclaimed Books, Box 18186,
Dallas, Texas 75218

Foreword

What can I say about Cookie, her life, and what she represents? God works in mysterious ways. The changes in her life have inspired many women and girls to acknowledge the power of the Lord and receive Jesus Christ into their lives. As I travel extensively across the country, I hear nothing but good reports of how marvelously God has used this young woman!

I remember the first time I met Cookie, and I can tell you that this book is the true story of a woman who was nothing but a broken shadow. But by the mercy of the Lord, her life has been put back together, stronger than ever.

I know that it has been very difficult for Cookie to be accepted by many, because of her particular ministry. But I have nothing but praise for her life, and for her husband, Demi, and the children. Cookie's program has ministered to hundreds of girls and women, many of whom no one else was able to reach or help.

I want you to read this book so we can praise the Lord together, for Cookie. I pray that its message will give you a true vision of the great things God can do by taking a "nobody" and making her into a "somebody", for His Glory.

COOKIE is a strong, human drama of a female who was hunting for self respect and identity. The only way she could find it was through Jesus Christ. My prayer is that as you read this book, God will speak very strongly to you. I praise God through Jesus Christ, for this great salvation.

Remember, Jesus loves you,
Nicky Cruz

Contents

CHAPTER 1

Prisoner of a Madman

"Silent Night, Holy Night. . ."

Somewhere church chimes were playing the heart-lifting carols, atuned with peace, goodwill and joy.

But in the dingy, sour-smelling room in which I'd allowed myself to be taken, the night was neither silent nor holy. Evil. . . that's what it was.

Christmas morning would soon be breaking, but in the room in which I'd stupidly let myself become entrapped, the night was one of evil and weeping. Instead of devoting the hallowed hours to carols and prayers, as people all over the city were doing, my companion, armed with his terrible knife, was devoting his time to sadism and perversion.

Sometimes, as the minutes dragged on, I screamed. Sometimes I wept. . .and sometimes, with a craftiness bred of desperation, I tried to soothe my tormentor. Stroking his forehead, my fingers sliding through perspiration, I'd croon to him hoping that, if he'd only relax, he'd fall asleep so that I could escape him.

But each time I thought he was about to let me go, he revived to a new fury, pressing his knife against me, forcing me to submit to the unspeakable.

Dimly, I heard the Christmas chimes, a counterpoint to my cries. The knife blade pricked my skin as my partner cursed me. So that I could live for another minute, I surrendered to his crazy desires. Yet, even at my most submissive, I was sure he was going to kill me.

"Silent Night. Holy Night.
All is calm. All is bright."

I couldn't remember when I'd felt calm or when I'd known a world filled with brightness.

"Well," I thought, "this man is going to kill me. Soon I will die, and if I do, perhaps it will be for the best." For, as a drug-addicted prostitute working the seamiest byways of New York to support my habit, I'd been as good as dead for years. Nobody would miss me anyway, not even my grandmother who'd loved me. . .not even my son, for I'd been nothing but trouble for the first, and I was a stranger to the second.

Yet, though I was spiritually dead and physically and mentally on the verge of death, my instinct for self-preservation was still alive and healthy, preventing me from tamely yielding to that threatening blade.

My dependence on drugs had brought me to this perilous situation, and even though my brain couldn't function properly anymore, I knew this was true—just as I knew that my habit would continue to fill my life with horror—if only I survived this Christmas eve!

If I'd had a pimp, he might have kept me away from the sick, strange men whose curious lusts make a cheap prostitute's profession so hazardous that she lives in perpetual fear.

But I'd never had a pimp, because I could scarcely

support one habit, much less two. And, besides, I was so ill mentally, physically and spiritually that the men who managed girls' street activities might have considered me more trouble than I'd be worth.

Scrawny, dirty and subject to hearing "voices," I'd been ordered out of one less-than-high-class bar from which I once operated. There's a great difference between being an expensive call girl and a fragment of the scum which clogs the ghettos and slums of New York.

Call girls live lives of sin and degradation. But prostitutes who do business on street corners suffer mental and physical abuse beyond description. And today some of these girls are scarcely into their teens. They are hard-faced, drug-addicted babies who'll do anything for five dollars.

Normally a New York prostitute works a neighborhood in which she's known, one with which she's familiar. And she insists that her tricks go to her room because she knows, from the horror stories she's heard and through experience of some of her peers, what can happen to a girl on strange turf.

However, on this particular Christmas eve, I was so desperate for a fix and potential tricks were so scarce that I'd foolishly ignored the rules.

There's no way to describe the hell a girl goes through when she's in the condition I was in. She doesn't just stand on a corner being a prostitute. She suffers incredible degradation and pain.

Anyway, it was on a Christmas eve in 1963, I believe, that my craving for a fix put me at the mercy of a madman. And though I obviously didn't know Jesus Christ at the time, I did realize what night it was because I could hear the church bells playing carols and because business was so rotten.

In a frenzy for a fix, I knew I would have to have money to get one, and I was out to try to turn a trick. My stomach was cramping so that I could hardly stand it yet, because of the cramping, I forced myself to go out looking for business.

A fix! I had to have one. A fix would make the cramps go away.

I must have looked awful, but even at my very best, it would have been hard to hustle a guy on Christmas eve because most of the men, even those usually found in bars, stay home with their wives and children on that night.

The ghetto bars that I usually worked were empty because, not only was it Christmas eve, but it was snowing. No potential customers were out drinking. I couldn't see hope for a dollar. Nobody, just nobody, was giving me a glance.

Because of the agonizing stomach pain, I thought I would have to sit down, or maybe even lie down. I was sick, sick.

I knew, though, that a fix would relieve me so, forgetting all the sordid stories I'd heard about what could happen to a prostitute in a strange neighborhood, I prowled beyond familiar territory, looking for any man who would give me money. . .under almost any condition.

Finally I came upon a bar that was packed, literally packed. I was afraid of hustling here where nobody knew me and where I had no idea of what the dangers might be. But my mania for drugs was greater than my fear so I went inside, and with little trouble at all, picked up a man.

Normally I would have insisted that he accompany me to a room I used regularly, paying a dollar a trick, where people in the building knew me and sort of kept an eye out for me and my associates.

But this man refused to go with me. "I'm not going to your place," he stubbornly insisted. "You and your people might rip me off when I get there. It might be a trap."

Talk about traps! I never envisioned the trap into which I'd be walking a few minutes later. Well, yes, I did realize the danger of working in strange territory, but had I foreseen that knife against my flesh, not even my agonizing desire for drugs would have driven me into that strange room. Or could it have forced me on? With such severe stomach cramps, perhaps I would have risked anything to find relief.

"I'll take you to my apartment," the man argued, "but I'm not going anywhere else."

An animal instinct caused me to be wary, warning me not to go with this strange man to a strange place. At the same time, my craving for drugs warned me too. . .that if I turned him down, I wouldn't be able to earn the price of a fix that night. I was so sick that nothing seemed to matter except my need for heroin. Finally I agreed, "Okay, let's go."

A prostitute's life is ghastly, at best, but when a girl needs a fix, turning a trick is worse than ever. Sex that's bought and paid for is always degrading, but it can be painful as well. However, I was so wild for the price of drugs that even the mention of another man going with us failed to make me back off.

"Okay." I mumbled, wondering how long it would be before I could get to my drug source.

The guy who joined us was as nice as anyone is likely to be when he buys a woman. As soon as he was through, he handed me the money and left.

In spite of the fact I was on strange territory, nothing so far was strange about the evening. I'd seen worse times in the room I rented.

But then, almost as soon as the door had closed behind the first man, the second had hit me. . .hard!

"What's the matter with you?" I yelled. "What are you doing? Are you crazy?"

He didn't answer. He only hit me again. . .and again. . .and again. He kept beating me until I crumpled to the floor—weak, cramping, still wild for a fix.

Then the man grabbed me, lifting me off the floor. He was crying! And so was I, because he was frightening and hurting me.

He carried me into the bathroom where he proceeded to throw me into the bathtub and wash me, hurting me still worse, all the while calling me a "no-good so-and-so." He was hurting me so that I screamed until I thought my lungs would burst.

Then he carried me back into the bedroom. Now he was holding a large butcher knife. "Do you see this?" he demanded. "I'm not going to let you leave here."

For hours he taunted and tortured me. As church bells rang out in celebration of the birth of Christ, he continued to assuage his sadistic appetite.

Once I managed to get halfway out the door before he caught me by the neck and threw me to the floor again.

"Please," I begged. "Don't you know that it's Christmas? I haven't seen my baby in a year. Please let me make a phone call and wish him a merry Christmas."

Amazingly, my tormentor agreed that would be all right. So I picked up the phone and dialed my grandmother who'd taken care of me as a little girl and was now taking care of my illegitimate son.

When she answered, I spoke calmly. "I just called to wish you a merry Christmas," I said. "Please kiss the baby for me."

"Where are you?" she wanted to know. Before I could say anything, the madman grabbed the phone, slammed down the receiver, and began to hit me again.

In between blows, between sweeps with the knife, sometimes he'd cry and call me names. I knew that he was totally crazy, homicidally so, and I wondered how many girls he'd already killed.

"Nobody is going to see you again, and nobody is going to miss you," he said.

"How many girls has this maniac killed?" I wondered again and again.

Then I thought of something else. If I could just get the knife, then I'd kill him. Yes, that's what I'd try to do. I'd knifed a person before, though not fatally, and I'd certainly rather kill him than let him kill me.

"Baby, baby," I crooned soothingly. If only I could find a way to grab that knife.

But my torturer, crazy as he was, was cunning. He never relaxed his guard. If he wasn't holding the knife tightly in his own hand, it was never within my reach.

At around 7:00 in the morning, as many families were homeward bound from early Christmas mass, the knife-wielder finally relaxed. His eyes closed. Could it be that he'd actually gone to sleep?

Despite that I'd earlier resolved to kill him if I got the chance, I only thought now of escape. So, stark naked, without taking time to put on a stitch, I ran out into the freezing Christmas morning.

The streets, assaulted during the night by a snow-storm, were icy as I ran totally nude toward 149th and Third Avenues. Church bells were ringing again—"Joy To The World," "Oh Come, All Ye Faithful"—as a cab pulled to the curb, its back door opened. The woman inside invited me to come in. Naked and battered, I was a frightening apparition.

Christ was acting through this woman as she threw her coat over me, shuddering at my bruises, and told the driver to take me to a hospital.

There doctors treated my injuries, but when they saw the needle marks, nobody suggested that I press charges against the man who'd injured me. For who'd believe the story of a drug-addicted prostitute? Not anybody. (Incidentally, I found out that the maniac worked for the post office.)

I knew I'd be out on the streets again the next day, because I would have to have more money. With a $200-a-day habit, what else could I do but hustle?

There would be no Christmas presents for me on that miserable morning. As I lay on the examination table being treated by a doctor turned hostile at the sight of my needle marks, I remembered my Shirley Temple doll. When I was a child, it had been a Christmas present, the finest and most beautiful I'd ever received.

It was so fine, I wasn't even allowed to play with it, but at least it was mine, and oh, how happy I'd been on the day I got that doll!

I hadn't been happy often—not even as a child, not even years ago when I was still "clean."

CHAPTER 2

Childhood Hustling

Puerto Rico is a land of bright flowers, glorious sunshine, charming people, and deplorable poverty.

Among its exports are rum, talented performers like Freddie Prinz and Henry Darrow (whose real name is Henrique Delgado), and paupers who flee to New York in search of a better life in the alleged land of opportunity.

Tourists trek to Puerto Rico to enjoy its Spanish colonial atmosphere, its warm beaches and gambling establishments.

At the time I got my Shirley Temple doll, my grandmother and I were living in a gambling establishment, though not one that tourists ever visited. In that little shack which was our home, the grandmother whom I called Abuelita ran what was called an "after hours joint."

During the day she worked for various well-to-do people, including the Catholic priest. But in order to survive, she increased our income by running the gambling hall.

My grandmother took care of me because my father, who would have been seventeen years old when I was born, had committed suicide before that unwanted event by drinking Lysol.

My mother, who was fourteen years old when I arrived, neither desired a baby nor had any idea what to do with one, so she gave me to my father's mother.

My grandmother, incidentally, had no men to help her because both my grandfathers were dead. One, like my father, had died after drinking Lysol, and the other had been killed by police.

So you can see that, by both heredity and environment, I seemed destined to be one of Society's outcasts.

Our house consisted of only one room, so my grandmother and I slept together.

While the gambling went on, my grandmother would post one or two men outside as lookouts, nonetheless the police raided us regularly.

One night during a raid, a pregnant woman who'd been gambling tried to get away. She fell, and both she and her baby died. That's what I remember most clearly about the raids—that woman falling, dying.

Although Abuelita operated a gambling joint, she was a strict and moral woman according to her point of view, and she was determined that I should have a better life than she has having.

Thin, almost emaciated, she wore her hair pulled back tightly into a bun and she viewed the world through deep-set eyes, burning with emotion.

Our house had no electricity and no icebox, and we would have had no food either, had Abuelita not worked all day and then operated a gambling game at night.

Because she wanted me to be superior to the other children in our barrio, she wouldn't let me play with them. In fact, she hardly let me out of the house, except during the Christmas season.

Although children in our village didn't expect Santa Claus to come, they did celebrate the visit of the Wise Men, and I'd join them in filling boxes with grass for the Three Kings' camels to eat. Even in our poor barrio, the Christmas season was a time for fiesta when the village would be filled with music, more like country-western than the traditional carols, but with a Nativity theme.

Musicians with guitars would go from house to house, at each door being offered good wishes and perhaps drinks. For everybody, even to the most miserably poor, was merry at Christmas. Children whose bellies were distended with hunger most of the year could look forward to special treats during the fiesta which commemorated the birth of Christ.

Then even our one-room shack was redolent with the rich aroma of pork, rice and beans, and a savory dish called pastel. Normally we couldn't enjoy such delicacies, but by scrimping throughout the year, Abuelita was able to prepare a feast at Christmas.

Unlike the others in our village, we even had a Christmas tree which was given us by one of the rich families my grandmother worked for. But, as far as I was concerned, this was a source of embarassment more than of pleasure. For the other village children, not too friendly anyway, resented this luxury item of ours.

On Christmas eve, my grandmother took me to midnight Mass but, even though I knew we were observing Jesus' birthday, I knew very little about the blessed baby and, because of my ignorance, cared even less. Mass was something I simply endured but didn't understand. I could say "Hail, Mary" and, after we went to the United States, made a point of saying it—both in English and Spanish—in case God wasn't bilingual.

Beyond that, religion meant nothing to me.

On the most memorable Christmas of my childhood, when I was about six years old, my grandmother gave me the Shirley Temple doll. One of the families she worked for had given her the money to buy it. She might have spent the money on something for herself or for something practical such as flour, but my Abuelita, loving me as she did, chose to buy the doll—more beautiful than any I'd ever seen.

No other child in the barrio had anything half so fine! Even more than our Christmas tree, the doll set me apart.

Since my grandmother cooked and cleaned for the priest, she was able to send me to a Catholic school attended by children from the the most respected families in town, and here I almost developed a split personality. Where the children in the barrio had resented me because we had a Christmas tree and because my grandmother wouldn't let me play with them, the children at the school ignored me because I was so poor.

Even if I'd been invited to their parties, I couldn't have gone, for I wouldn't have had the right clothes. But I wasn't invited, and that hurt. My classmates didn't insult me openly, but they slighted me in subtle ways until a scar tissue formed over my psychological wounds.

By the time I was seven, my attitude was both cynical and defiant. I was hostile and defensive, not only with my affluent classmates but with my teachers who, I was sure, preferred the other children to me.

And so I began to dream two dreams, each directly opposed to the other. Thus I began to develop two personalities, both growing out of my hatred for the poverty in which I existed, the ugliness of our dusty village street and our one-room house.

Somewhere in patios, bright and sweet-smelling with flowers, people laughed, relaxed, and wore pretty clothes.

But there was little rest and laughter in my neighborhood, and precious few sweet smells. Instead there were flies and dogs and drudgery and hunger. And I hated it. How I hated it!

Someday, I promised myself, I'd move into another world. Someday, according to one of my dreams, I'd be a teacher.

Yes, that's what I'd be. I'd walk proudly through town, respected by everyone—even the rich parents who'd send their children to learn from me. Even the priest and the nuns would admire the way I presided over my classroom.

People would ask my opinion on this subject and that. And I'd never again live in our barrio.

When I dreamt my respectable dream, I also saw myself as a bride, virginal, clothed in all white, proving to the world that I was a good girl as I marched down the aisle to meet my bridegroom. Coming from a family with a criminal record, I felt an urgent need to prove my personal purity someday.

My other dream was more colorful but less commendable because, in it, I saw myself as a lady of the evening.

The phrase "lady of the evening" is an euphemism but more applicable to my dream than the word "prostitute" because, by that time, I knew what a prostitute did to earn money, and that phase of the lifestyle didn't appeal to me.

However, I knew of a house in which a number of women lived, all of whom dressed dazzlingly in my opinion and all of whom enjoyed enviable freedom. I, who lived only thirty minutes away from San Juan, had never seen the capital city, yet I'd hear these women talk about going to San Juan as casually as I spoke of going to school. I, who had never been in an automobile, saw them climb in and out of fine cars regularly.

And I was jealous. I wanted to ride in long, powerful automobiles. I wanted to travel. And I wanted the independence these women enjoyed.

Life in our barrio was so restricted that no woman in the community, other than one of these flashy ladies, would dare to smoke or wear slacks or makeup.

When my grandmother earned extra money cooking for a Rotary Club banquet or some similar event, she'd make me stay with her in the kitchen sitting as still as a mouse in a straight chair, protected by her formidable presence from the evil that might befall me were I to wander into the banquet room full of men. She insisted that my appearance be demure and, no matter where my thoughts might stray, she kept me as physically restricted as possible, considering the fact that she usually had to leave me when she worked.

Her influence was so strong that, even when I was hustling on the streets of New York, I wore little makeup.

When I envied those women who rode in cars and had so much money to spend, when I dreamt of being one of them, I only wanted to enjoy their freedom and wealth. I didn't want to do everything that they did.

Yet, shockingly, before I was ten years old, an age when most little girls are Brownie Scouts, I was doing almost what these women did.

Blas was the janitor of the school I attended, and I'm sure he knew I was poor. In any case, he offered me two dollars one day if I'd go with him to the basement.

I wanted those two dollars. Oh my, yes, how I wanted the money! Still, I didn't want to go to the basement with the maintenance man because I had an idea that something bad might happen and, despite my envy of the fun-loving ladies in the flashy clothes, I really didn't want to do anything bad.

Momentarily, I'd even thought of being a nun, although I didn't especially like the nuns I knew. Still, like teachers, they were respected, so I thought fleetingly it might be nice to be like one. But how in the world could I ever become a bride of Christ if I were going into the basement doing bad things with the school janitor?

My two divergent personalities were warring within me. I did honestly and truly want to be the good girl Abuelita expected me to be; yet at the same time, I did hate being poor, and I did want those two dollars.

In the end I went to the basement with Blas who led me into the bathroom and ran his hands over my body. His coarse fondling was repulsive at first but, since he did nothing more than touch me and since I still wanted the two dollars, I didn't run away.

At last he gave me the money and told me I could go home, warning me rather needlessly not to tell anyone where I'd acquired my new wealth.

I had no intention of telling anyone! I felt dirty as I left him but I also felt happy because I was temporarily rich and, by the time I got home, I was in quite high spirits.

"Look, Abuelita," I told my grandmother as I skipped in the door, "I found two dollars in the street."

"That's wonderful," she said, taking the precious banknotes. She was as happy as I, not doubting in the least that I'd actually found the money just as I claimed.

My encounter with the maintenance man hadn't been pleasant but it hadn't been unpleasant enough to reject his next invitation to the basement. As a matter of fact, I went with him into that basement every Saturday for two years, and permitted him to paw my body in exchange for two dollars.

If my grandmother ever wondered how I happened to find this exact amount of money every Saturday, she never said anything about it. We needed the money so badly that she probably forced herself into believing I'd come by it through some good luck. And besides, as young as I was, she would never imagine I was practicing something so close to prostitution.

During the two years that I was selling myself to the maintenance man, I went regularly to Confession as my school required me to do. But I never confessed what was going on in the basement because I didn't think it was a sin.

In fact, after that first episode with Blas, I no longer felt guilty at all for allowing him to pet me for a price. I didn't even feel guilty about lying to Abuelita.

Despite the instruction I was getting from the nuns, I knew even less about Jesus at this point than I did about life on Mars.

CHAPTER 3

Promised Land

At the age of twelve, I finally got to see San Juan. Abuelita had decided we should move to New York, which we reached by way of the San Juan airport. My loving, fierce, hard-working little grandmother, hardly bigger than a wren but with hopes for me bigger than all outdoors, had heard that New York was a latter day Eden, a city rich with opportunities for all.

My uncle and his family had lived there for some time and sent back such exciting reports of new life in this "land of plenty" that my grandmother had been saving money for years in hopes of being able to join them there.

Most of the time I put her plans into the fantasy category, like my fleeting notion that I might eventually become a nun. Then one day Abuelita broke the astounding news: New York was no longer just a place she dreamed of. It was the city to which we were going to move immediately. Through incessant drudgery and scrimping, she'd saved the price of two plane tickets, plus a bit more. So we would actually fly away to the land of everlasting bounty and happiness.

"We'll do much better there," she promised. "We may even get rich."

It was hard enough for me to believe we were actually going to New York, much less that we might become wealthy. However, if Abuelita were about to make the first part of her long-range plan a reality, who could tell? Perhaps she could make the rest of her dream come true as well.

Or could she?

I'd wanted to travel—to escape our barrio—but now, as we were about to go, the familiar poverty became almost dear to me. Oddly enough, I wanted to stay right where I was. Instead of envying the flashily dressed ladies of their travel, I now envied them because they didn't have to leave our village. . not unless they really wanted to.

As far as Abuelita was concerned, the plane which bore us from San Juan to New York was a motorized magic carpet. Her excitement was so intense that it should have been infectuous but for some reason I felt lethargic.

"Just think," Abuelita chattered, "we'll be in New York in just a few hours." Yet somehow the prophecy didn't delight me. For reasons which I couldn't analyze, New York frightened me and, had I been able to foresee my first few years there, I would have been even more afraid. In fact, I would have been more afraid had I been able to envision only the next few hours, for the New York in which we landed was a grey, hostile city filled with people whose language I couldn't understand and who, if they noticed me at all, looked at me coldly. "One more Puerto Rican trying to get on the gravy train."

That's all I meant to most of those who met our

incoming flight. We were hardly a welcome addition to the city, Abuelita and I.

The clash of truck gears grinding their way through congested streets, the cries of cabbies shouting unpleasantly at other drivers, the noise of people, people, people—all jabbering incomprehensibly— alarmed me so that I wished for Puerto Rico's quiet, jungle-green hills. I already missed the clear sunshine and the flowers.

Why, I wouldn't have thought such a thing could be possible but I even missed our one-room shack and the drabness of the barrio.

Abuelita and I moved into a one-room apartment with my uncle, two aunts, and four cousins. Our quarters did have electricity and running water, conveniences that our former home had lacked, but to my twelve-year-old mind the apartment suffered in comparison to our village hovel.

In Puerto Rico, Abuelita and I had lived in a single room but only two of us had shared it and rather than being crammed high in a building, packed closely among other buildings, it had stood alone with fresh air just outside the door.

Actually, the neighborhood in which we'd settled wasn't so bad. Quite the reverse. Well-to-do families whose apartments boasted several rooms lived close at hand so that when my grandmother enrolled me in the nearest Catholic school, my classmates weren't tough street urchins. They were well-behaved, neatly dressed, upper middle-class children who had never rubbed shoulders with a Puerto Rican before and thus found my inability to speak English, exotic.

So, for awhile, I was accepted after a fashion by my peers. Children can communicate without language so, through the games that we played and the smiles we exchanged, some of my schoolmates and I became friends. Or so I believed.

But after two of them visited our crowded apartment and viewed the circumstances in which I lived, they dropped me. After that, my "new friends" would have nothing more to do with me, except for occasionally making me the object of a joke.

I was at an age which is particularly hard on girls, at best. With my body changing, I was plagued by strange sensations and desires, as well as the perfectly normal universally shared desire to have friends—to be liked.

Instead, I was an outcast. Like Ruth of the Old Testament standing midst the alien corn, I was in an alien environment with even my own body becoming alien to me. And to make matters worse, I, who had always been a good student, had been put back a grade in school.

Oh how I hated New York and the unfathomable language its residents spoke. Had I realized that many of those residents had only spoken English for a little while and at first found the tongue as strange as I found it, this might have been of comfort, for then I would have realized I was part of a group larger than my immediate Puerto Rican family.

But I didn't know this. Outside our apartment, I felt totally isolated, immeasurably miserable.

Finally, from two sources, I was able to gain some sense of belonging. One was a nun, patient and perceptive; the other was a street gang—armed to the teeth and willing to kill!

I met the Sister at the first school I attended in New York, and the gang in another.

The nun had visited Puerto Rico, knew some Spanish, and felt that we could help each other through language lessons. So after the regular school day ended, she worked with me, teaching me basic English while, hopefully, she improved her Spanish. As a result, I began to speak and comprehend a little of the language I heard around me so that I was not quite the outcast I had been.

I was introduced to gang culture at the second Catholic school I attended in New York—St. Cecilia's. It was an ugly place, infected with ugly activity, including gang warfare. However, I didn't actually join a gang there. I became part of a gang only after enrolling in my first public school, where I was forced to fight for my life during a violent interracial brawl.

CHAPTER 4

I Become a Racist

Girls in the Catholic school I attended in Puerto Rico were sedate and chaste. Students at the first Catholic school I attended were well-behaved. But Girls at the second school I attended in New York were more chased than chaste. . .boys all but attacked them in the halls. And they actually enjoyed it.

I changed schools when Abuelita, our numerous relatives and I moved from our one-room apartment to more spacious accomodations in Spanish Harlem. Using my limited English, I had dickered for a five-room flat which Abuelita had to "buy" for $300 before she could rent it for $100 a month.

Considering what we got, the price was outrageous, but at first the new apartment seemed like Heaven on earth because, not only did it provide a modicum of privacy for me, it was in a Puerto Rican neighborhood where the neighbors spoke our language, in every sense of the word.

Still there was a drawback attached to our new place of residence. With a new address, I was required to attend a different school—St. Cecelia's. And although it was a Catholic institution, its students' only religion was that of the streets. All they honored was toughness, the ability to survive. They were alley-wise, foul-mouthed, sexually precocious and indifferent to formal education, flaunting faculty control to the extent of necking in public and fighting when and where they pleased.

The building which housed St. Cecelia's was appropriate to the student body—dingy, disfigured with pornographic graffiti and generally depressing.

In Puerto Rico, I'd never seen a woman smoke in public unless she was a whore, but at my new school it was a common practice for girls to smoke in the restrooms. Most of my classmates there shocked and alarmed me, but the ones who truly terrified me were the gang members.

They were easy to recognize by their vocabulary, costuming and attitudes. The boys wore their hair in heavily-oiled ducktails and jellyrolls. Their chests were either covered by tee shirts which fit the skin to show off muscles the wearer might have or they were exposed by gaudy shirts unbuttoned to the navel. Trousers were worn so low and so tight that they must have been crotch-pinchingly painful.

Gang members looked dangerous and were. Sometimes rival gangs warred with each other—in school as well as out—filling me with such dread that I carefully avoided all factions. Trying hard to be invisible, I hoped that if I left the gangs alone they would do the same for me.

If I'd stayed at St. Cecelia's, as bad as it was, I might have avoided becoming a gang member. But I'd hardly been there a month when I had to change schools again.

Once again, a move was the reason for transfer.

If my inability to speak English adequately had caused problems for me, Abuelita's inability to speak it at all had caused worse ones for both of us because, due to her language handicap, she couldn't find work and soon spent all her savings.

When that happened, my uncle, now a loving Christian but then considerably less, tossed us out, leaving us to sleep on the streets of the Bowery. We were literally on the sidewalk, without so much as a pillow between ourselves and the pavement.

Oh, how I longed for our barrio and one-room shack during that uncomfortable, fear-filled night. New York, up to that point, had held nothing but disappointment and, although I wasn't yet aware, it was going to get worse.

After a night of sleeping on the sidewalk, a slum family showing more charity than our relatives took us in and explained that we were eligible for welfare, which was certainly an understatement in our case. Since we were totally without possessions or means, Abuelita had no trouble in getting on the welfare rolls.

Many people who've never lived on welfare payments imagine that recipients loll about in comfort at the taxpayers' expense. Having lived on welfare, though, I know this can't be true, for a person whose only income is a welfare check is too poorly nourished to be comfortable. And, as for lolling. . .well. . most welfare recipients secretly hold jobs in order to survive.

To live on welfare payments alone is to starve. So Abuelita became one of the sly ones. As she'd done in Puerto Rico when she ran a gambling establishment to give us money to eat, she began to break the law. She accepted such work as she could find but didn't report it to the welfare authorities for fear we'd lose the small, monthly check they sent us. This deception didn't hurt her conscience at all, for she'd

learned that in the new land, as well as the old, we had
to be crafty if we were to save ourselves.

Still, Abuelita remained the basically moral
woman she'd always been, stubbornly determined
that I be educated and upright. She was as fiercely
protective toward me as ever and would have
been appalled by the conduct of my classmates at St.
Cecelia's.

Since most of the work she found was babysitting
and as the children she tended called her Nina (the
Spanish equivalent of Nana), I began to call her Nina
too.

In our reduced circumstances, we located another
place to live, a thoroughly undesirable one because it
was in an undesirable area, West Harlem. Although
the residents of our new neighborhood were no
poorer than those of Spanish Harlem, and certainly
no poorer than our neighbors in Puerto Rico had
been, their streets were more dangerous—both
spiritually and physically—than other streets I'd
known. For the byways of West Harlem reeked with
a contagious hatred. "Spick," "Nigger"—these
were two of the more polite terms by which neighbors
addressed one another. Usually the salutations were
even more obscene.

Blacks and Puerto Ricans shared West Harlem
and, in their mutual despair, turned on each other.
The blacks, embittered by their own suffering, had a
compulsive need to lash out at somebody, and the
Puerto Ricans were a convenient target, while the
Puerto Ricans exercised their own frustration
through attacks on the blacks. In our mutually
shared ghetto, two sets of losers learned to loathe
each other—to loathe and to fear.

I'd never felt prejudice, much less hate, toward a
group before, but having enrolled in my first public

school, I discovered the feeling of racial hatred for the first time. We hate what we fear and I was afraid of the black students who were openly hostile toward me.

I talked Nina into letting me transfer from St. Cecelia's to Booker T. Washington Junior High School because the language requirements there were more relaxed, and I could move forward a grade. But although I liked being in the grade I would have been in Puerto Rico, I didn't like anything else about my new school environment. Booker T. Washington School could rightfully be called an institution of learning but what students learned there was how to hate and maim.

The maiming was psychological as well as physical for, in the musty hallways and the bleak schoolyard where gangs representing racial factions attacked each other, students received more than surface scars. Many were injected with prejudices which will fester within them the rest of their lives, to become more crippling than broken bones.

The blacks and Puerto Ricans should have stuck together at Booker T. Washington because, even united, they were still outnumbered by other ethnic groups. A great number of students were Irish, the boys being as tough and filled with macho pride as the non-whites. They, like the Puerto Ricans and the blacks, had their gangs—armed and ready to fight at the drop of an insult.

The Irish, the Puerto Ricans and the blacks, were united in only one respect. All three groups disliked the fourth and majority element in the student body— the Jews. They were so smart that everybody detested them.

The Jews didn't join gangs, not even in self-defense, but peered earnestly at their books through their glasses, which seemed to be a racial badge. Almost every Jewish student at Booker T. Washington wore glasses, just as every one of them quietly and determinedly made top grades.

But in the opinion of the other students, they were disgusting.

Pressured by the presence of the Jewish majority and abetted by the presence of the even fairer-skinned Irish, the dusky Puerto Ricans and blacks temporarily united. It was during such a truce that I scored a personal triumph.

Though the school was named for Booker T. Washington, a famous black American, no black had ever been elected president of the student body.

Each year every candidate for this high office presented an assembly program as a highlight of his political campaign.

One year, in support of a black candidate, I choreographed and performed a dance number to the song "Blue Moon." I was a self-taught but effective interpretive dancer so I assembled a group of Puerto Rican girls and taught them a routine. We made our own costumes, all blue, and staged such a well-received assembly program that our candidate was elected.

His victory was a triumph for interracial cooperation, but more often interracial strife was the order of the day at Booker T. Washington.

Though I was constantly tormented and insulted, I avoided gangs and stayed out of fights for a long period. But at Booker T. Washington it seemed that only the Jews could be neutral forever. I needed a gang to protect me but I didn't discover how badly until the day I found myself surrounded by an ominous wall of blacks. They were intent upon vengeance because of what I'd done to one of their own—a hulking, vulgar, girl named Norma who had made my life miserable from the time we'd first met.

Until this particular day, I had forced myself to ignore her insults and harassment, because she was twice my size and I was afraid of her. But eventually my self-control had snapped and I had answered her insults in kind. Almost.

Actually, by Booker T. Washington Junior High School standards, my reply had been mild. But Norma, misunderstanding me, thought I'd called her a "nigger" and, in a fury, she'd flung herself at me, right in the classroom, beating me with her fists until I'd instinctively struck back.

Her hands were huge and solid, like great hammers pounding upon me. Reacting to the pain of the blows, to the overwhelming presence of her oversized body and the fetid skin smell which sickened me as she shoved against me, I fought viciously. Though much smaller than Norma, I was agile enough to get in a few solid blows of my own, one of which knocked off her glasses. When I heard them hit the floor, without thinking, I stepped on the lenses, grinding them under my heel.

Norma, screaming with rage, intensified her assault.

Meanwhile, the teacher had joined the battle and, since he was even bigger than Norma, he managed to separate us.

Back at my desk with adrenalin no longer pumping, I was sick with apprehension. I'd held my own in a fight with Norma but I knew that I'd survived only a battle, not a war. I would have to pay for my foolhardiness. I knew it!

Sure enough, that very afternoon as I tried to leave school, I found myself blocked by Norma and her gang. Taunting, grinning, threatening, they surrounded me. There was no way through or around them. Were they going to kill me? Terrified, I wondered.

I didn't pray, because I didn't know how. Instead, I steeled myself for what might be a battle to the death.

CHAPTER 5

Gang Deb

The gang members didn't intend to kill me—only to give me a terrific scare and the beating of my life.

They amply succeeded in the first for, as we faced each other, I was almost paralyzed with fear. My stomach knotted and for a second I thought I'd vomit up the bile which was scorching my throat.

But before I could vomit or beg or cringe, hate saved my self-respect. Suddenly I was more furious than afraid. A venomous rage took hold of my body and mind so that, like a robot, without quite realizing what I was doing, I threw myself at my assailants.

I'd been such a subdued student during most of my tenure at Booker T. Washington that my violence must have taken Norma and her friends by surprise. But their surprise wasn't enough to help me much.

I was outnumbered many to one, yet fighting like a demon, my arms and legs flailing, I gave as many bruises as I received. Tactics never entered my mind. I only thought of hitting, hitting, hurting and hurting, and—finally—escaping.

Some soldiers who've been in combat say that a bullet doesn't hurt at the instant of impact. The agony comes later. During combat, men have actually lost arms without realizing it for several seconds. When the brain is consumed with the problems of survival, it's slow to register physical pain.

I know this is true because, as I grappled with Norma and her gang, I scarcely felt their blows. I was cut, I was bruised, I was bloody. But I was fighting so hard it didn't matter. With the fury of a fiend, I not only defended myself, I attacked until at last the black wall crumbled before me and disappeared.

I was alive. I was free. I could go home. Pushing my hair out of my eyes, dabbing at a trickle of blood that was running down my shin, straightening my sadly disarranged skirt and petticoats, I noticed for the first time that a crowd had gathered to watch the melee.

Not one person had tried to help me, but many had seen and, as it turned out, had inwardly applauded my wild defense. After the fight, I was able to walk down the school's corridors and on its campus with newly acquired safety. For the word was out:

"That girl is little, but she's mean. She's a great fighter. You should see her when she's mad!"

The student body began treating me with more respect and pretty soon I was accorded a major compliment according to Booker T. Washington standards for, when I was fourteen, I was accepted as a Diamond "deb." (The Diamonds were a Puerto Rican gang, and the "debs" were their ladies' auxiliary, so to speak.)

Approximately one hundred strong, the Diamonds were street-hardened boys between twelve and eighteen years old, each equipped with a highly sensitive notion of honor and a weapon ever ready to defend it. The gang's only reason for being was to protect its own—its members and its territory—from assault and/or insult, real or imagined.

The Diamonds wore chips on their shoulders and knives or zip guns elsewhere, and the combination resulted in repeated "rumbles," some of which were fatal.

A gang member spent most of his time either fighting, planning a fight, or recovering from a fight. And the same applied to the "debs."

While a gang member's business was to fight, his pleasure was to party and, like college fraternity initiates, the Booker T. Washington students socialized within their clearly defined groups, though one gang's parties were much like the other, with entertainment consisting of necking, getting drunk on cheap wine, and dancing to rock music in a dimly lighted room—in approximately that order.

At this time, drugs weren't a part of the scene, so I was getting my "high" from Ripple or something similar. I'd gone into gang life as a girl who was comparatively naive, a virgin who didn't really like to fight and who, though I would never admit to my new friends, still hoped to be a teacher.

A teacher? If the Diamonds and their "debs" had realized that a would-be "teach" was in their midst, they would have booted me out of their circle. And once again I would have been a frightened loner, a misfit in a still-strange and cruel city.

I couldn't let that happen. I couldn't let my peers suspect that I was less than hard as nails. So I began drinking and necking and taking on the characteristics of the group. I was talking tough and looking cheap.

Under gang tutelege, I changed quickly, at least on the surface. I learned to be so vicious in a fight that I soon became a deb leader, hated and feared by students who weren't Diamonds. Worse than that, I came to enjoy this dark prestige. I, who'd been afraid for so long, found pleasure in recognizing the fear in others who obviously went out of their way to avoid trouble with me.

My appearance changed too. . .to Nina's dismay, I no longer wore dresses to school but rather tight-fitting skirts and a leather jacket, which she detested. "You look like one of those cheap girls who belongs to a gang," she would scold.

Yet, at the same time, she remained proud of me, confident that I was a good girl who was preparing for a life much better than hers had been. She never suspected (nor did I at fourteen) that I was paving the way for a life of hard drug addiction, borderline madness and sexual promiscuity which I would partially spend in mental institutions and jails.

Nina's scoldings irritated me, but her recurring declaration that I was a "good girl" irritated me even more. Didn't she realize the very phrase "a good girl" was a joke! Nina, to me, was a joke. Her old fashioned ideas were laughable—both laughable and maddening. A girl who lived according to Nina's lights had no fun, no friends, no protection in the sordid confines of the Booker T. Washington student body. Couldn't Nina understand an obvious thing like that? What was the matter with my stupid little grandmother? The love I'd felt for Nina was slowly being replaced with scorn.

I was becoming much closer to the gang than to my grandmother. She who had protected me for so long was being replaced by the Diamonds who offered the kind of protection she couldn't supply and didn't realize I even needed.

However, when I was in the eighth grade, I lost my

status with the Diamonds and thus the sense of security they'd provided.

One day at school I tried to go into the lunchroom through the wrong line and, when a black monitor had rightfully tried to stop me, the Diamond I was with brandished a zip gun.

According to the gang code, no Diamond was to accept rebuff from anybody. Pedro, the boy I was with, hadn't intended to shoot the monitor, only to scare him, but he did fire the gun and the ricocheting bullet lodged in the black boy's arm. Fortunately for him (and for Pedro), the wound wasn't terribly serious, but its results were for me.

My Diamond escort and I were questioned about the incident and, though I was exonerated, he was sent to jail. And, at that, my own gang turned on me! The Diamonds, without asking to hear my side of the story, assumed that I'd given evidence against Pedro to save myself and, according to their system of justice, I had to be punished. Severely.

I was so frightened—so afraid of my former friends—that even Nina realized that I was living in terror and, to protect me from the Diamonds, moved to another apartment seven blocks away, out of the gang territory. No Diamond would likely invade another gang's turf, so I was safe but in exile until Pedro got out of jail to clear me.

During this period, I stayed out of school, not only out of fear but because I'd been suspended.

When I returned to classes, the Diamonds and their debs accepted me, though only tentatively, for they weren't quite sure of me. I, most certainly, was no longer sure of them. I'd seen the boys and girls whom I considered my friends turn on me without giving me a chance to explain, so I never felt entirely secure with the Diamonds again.

Nevertheless, I continued to cut classes with the gang, to get drunk with them, and to embrace the Diamond's violent code which boiled down to this:

If you're attacked psychologically or physically, strike back—hard.

The idea of turning the other cheek was totally foreign to gang members. And it was this deadly eye-for-an-eye, tooth-for-a-tooth philosophy which finally put me out of school again and almost into my grave.

But instead of landing in my grave, it landed me in Bellevue. I was going downhill fast and my descent was about to pick up speed for, before I was sixteen, I was to be incarcerated in a crazy house and introduced to heroin and raped.

I was also to become a near-suicide victim.

CHAPTER 6

Heroin, Rape and the Gate to Hell

My suicide attempt and trip to Bellevue grew indirectly out of a fight which grew directly out of my devotion to the Diamond code.

Because I had enough native intelligence to make good grades in everything except conduct, most of my teachers still thought there was hope for me.

However, one disagreed. She loathed gang members and could find nothing good in a Diamond deb. She disliked me, particularly, perhaps because she realized that I had some potential, and it angered her to see me wasting it. She regularly rebuked me in front of the class and on one day told me to stand in a corner.

Well, nobody was about to make a Diamond deb do a thing like that! The gang mentality would never permit it. So I said that I wouldn't stand in the corner, whereupon the teacher tried to put me there by force. Conditioned as I was to meeting force with force, I reacted by kicking her, and a noisy struggle ensued.

To the delight of the class, the teacher attempted to drag me across the room while I kicked her until her shins bled. She was stronger than I'd expected but I was strong too, so we were pretty evenly matched. I grew uncontrollably violent for, to me, the teacher represented everything bad that had happened in my life—every setback and disappointment.

I was suspended for a period of time and, during my period of punishment, I became so despondent that I tried to kill myself. Or I told myself that was what I was trying to do. Maybe I was only trying to frighten Nina and my teachers because I didn't drink a sure poison as my father had done or throw myself under a subway train. Instead I sought death through less certain means—an overdose of aspirin.

Nina found me unconscious on the floor and, when I came to, I was in Bellevue. The doctors there assured Nina that I would live and, because she demanded the information, they also assured her that I was still a virgin. This phase of the examination had humiliated and enraged me.

I was bitterly hurt that Nina could doubt my virginity. And I was agonizingly embarassed by the procedure which confirmed my maidenhood. How dare Nina! How dare the doctors! It's not surprising that Nina had finally lost confidence in my character. But even though I'd become mean, foul-mouthed and disrespectful of all authority, I was nonetheless determined to marry in a white dress, reminding myself over and over again that I was too smart to follow the pitiful examples of girls I knew who'd found themselves pregnant in junior high school.

I wanted the boys in the gang to respect me—not just use me. Somehow I was still convinced that I was a special person with a special future in store, not as a nun but maybe—just maybe—I might yet be a teacher. This ambition, of course, I was careful to keep secret from the gang.

My violence had been bred of insult and poverty—

not of drugs. My mind and body were still my own. The first hadn't been claimed by dope, nor the second by a lusty Diamond.

However, all that was about to change for, when I came out of Bellevue, I found my friends enjoying a new kick—marijuana. And while I didn't like the effect it seemed to be having on them, I began using it too.

Physically marijuana isn't addictive, or so I've been told, but psychologically it can have a damaging effect, as I soon found out once I started depending on it to get me through each day. The hazy comfort I drew from each joint kept me from having to worry, to think, or to try. Stoned on pot, I could drift through the hours, ignoring hardships and responsibility.

Meanwhile, some of the Diamonds were discovering a new escape. After being introduced to the drug culture by marijuana, they progressed to heroin and became a grim object lesson for me. Not yet mainliners, they relied on snorts of heroin for their highs but, when I saw them in such strange, sleepy, out of control condition, I was repelled. If heroin could change a person that much, I thought, I didn't want to fool with the stuff. Marijuana made me feel terrific, and that was drug enough for me. I wanted no part of the deadly "horse."

Yes, that's what I told myself, but pretty soon curiosity began corroding my resolve.

A boy from our hometown in Puerto Rico came to New York and, though he was a junkie—and junkies usually turned me off—I accepted him like a member of the family. At first, I'd hated his habit but gradually I began to accept his addiction and to wonder how he felt when he was high. What were the "wonderful" effects of the stuff which made it so indispensable to him?

If my junkie friends had been true friends, they would have warned me: "It's death. Keep away."

But few heroin users (or users of any hard drugs, for that matter) have any compunction about introducing others to their deadly habit. And so it was the boy from our Puerto Rican village, the one I held almost as dear as a brother, who gave me my first snort of horse.

However, he did so at my urging.

He came to me one day to beg for my little radio, my most precious possession, by far. "Just let me borrow it," he begged. "You'll get it back, I just have to have something for a fix. I've just got to have a fix. Please, let me have the radio."

I didn't want to let him have the radio because I was sure I'd never see it again and it, like pot, was a means of escape from the ugly streets, ugly school rooms, and from the ugliness of my life in general. I could turn it on and be transported, via music, right out of the real world.

"Give me the radio," he insisted, in a tone that combined a plea with a threat. "Please. I've got to have it."

I looked at my cherished radio, reluctant to give it away, since I knew that's what the loan would amount to. But a daring idea was forming in my head, so I handed it to him.

"All right. You can have the radio to exchange for a fix," I consented, "if you'll share your stuff with me. A little pinch is all I'll want. Is that okay?"

Caguita (so called for our mutual hometown, Caguas) was in no condition to argue, and, shortly after he left with my radio, he was back with the heroin.

My high was so intense and so gratifying that, once I'd come down, I could understand how deadly the drug could be and how easily I might become an addict. So, for several months I avoided the stuff, smugly believing that I had used heroin, only through curiosity, for the first and last time.

That's what I told myself, but how wrong I was! Eventually I would give in to the temptation to use it once more. "Just one more time," I was thinking, remembering the exquisite pleasure I'd derived from my first snort, "I tried heroin once months ago and I haven't needed it since, so that proves I can take it or leave it."

"Just one more time won't hurt me."

So again I tried heroin. . .and again. . .and again. Whether I would admit it to myself or not, I was heading toward addiction. Two catastrophes were driving me in that direction, both of which I had brought on myself.

First, I'd failed algebra and, as a result, lost my chance at taking college preparatory high school courses. Now there would be no way I could become a teacher.

Possibly because of my language handicap, I didn't understand algebra at all and because of my dedication to the Diamond code, I refused to ask for help with that difficult subject.

I couldn't help the fact I didn't understand English perfectly, but I alone was to blame for the fact that I put the gang code ahead of passing an important subject. No gang member would ask a teacher for tutoring. To do so would be to lose face.

So, although I knew I was failing algebra, I stubbornly resisted the weak impulse to ask my teacher for help. I failed the course as a consequence, and was transferred from the academic program to Central Commercial High School, a vocational school for girls.

Reacting to this disappointment, I became a worse discipline problem than ever. I no longer had any ambition. Knowing I couldn't be a teacher, I had no purpose in life and nothing to anticipate except drab, miserable poverty.

At fifteen, I had no further reason for going to school at all, so I cut classes frequently and upset the ones I did attend with my gutter language and hostile behavior.

Shortly afterward, I was raped, and this, again, was at least partly my own fault. I'd never been closely involved with a fellow so, despite the sexual activity of my friends, I was still so naive that I stupidly invited trouble.

My social activity consisted of drinking and smoking pot with the gang, and through these sessions, I met a twenty-four year old soldier who seemed quite taken with me. I didn't find him particularly attractive, but I was flattered by the attentions of this older man. He was full grown, not a silly boy. He knew something of the world, I thought, so I should be pleased that he chose me to maul and paw.

Frankly, I led him on. Teasingly, I allowed him liberties up to a point, foolishly believing that I could control him when I decided to.

But the fact that we were necking while stoned made it unlikely that I could control myself—much less my partner. Nevertheless, I hadn't the slightest intention of losing my virginity to this stocky, young man whose complexion was no better than his morals. Too inexperienced sexually to realize I was actually inviting rape, I only understood the danger after it was too late.

Overpowered, I was robbed forever of my chance to wear a white wedding gown. Apparently I was as cheap and worthless as the worst of my peers, so why should I try to be more than I was?

That's what I asked myself as I gave up all thoughts of respectability. Unable to stand myself or my life, I sought escape through both liquor and drugs.

I even introduced some of my classmates to drugs, and this was a mistake which, in turn, introduced me to new horrors.

Caught supplying dope to fellow students, I was very nearly sent to a reformatory because, at this point, not even my most loving adherent (and I only had one) could find much good in me. Instead of an asset to Society, I'd become a threat.

Still Nina—good ole Nina—remained loyal. Clinging to the naive notion that there was yet hope for me, she helped me convince the court that I wasn't delinquent, only disturbed. So, instead of being sent to a prison for juveniles, I was sent to a hospital for all kinds—just so the kinds had been adjudged crazy!

My punishment consisted of being committed to Rockland State Hospital, a mental institution, where for the first time I was introduced to lesbianism.

CHAPTER 7

Introduction to the Mad House

Most attendants at institutions for women are lesbians. Since no daintily feminine woman could handle the inmates, personnel must necessarily be big, muscular and masculine-looking.

I've been a patient at Rockland State seven times and during those periods of incarceration when I was helpless and dependent upon the attendants for any consideration I was to get, for small kindnesses I needed, I learned to tolerate lesbianism, in order to stay sane. I have never approved of it but, at the mercy of Rockland's staff, my tolerance of lesbian activity kept me from going as crazy as the craziest there.

This may be difficult to explain to a person who's never been committed to a state mental hospital but, while I disapproved of lesbianism, at Rockland I reached a state where I enjoyed minor lesbian contact, because I'd grown so hungry for human affection that a hug or a pat from anyone, a woman included, made me feel better. When women are denied love by the world, they may turn to each other, not necessarily for sexual excitement but simply for assurance that somebody cares.

44

A large percentage of prostitutes are lesbians who have been driven into relationships with other women through the brutality of men. A friend of mine, hooked on drugs as an adolescent, was exploited by her own grandfather who, knowing of her need for money to support her habit, paid her for sexual privileges. Her male cousins used her in the same manner until the girl, in order to escape from her lascivious family, became a New York prostitute.

By this time, not surprisingly, she'd come to dislike men intensely. Yet she wanted and needed affection—affection and tenderness—which she eventually found with a lesbian lover.

And this girl's story is not an unusual one.

When I first saw Rockland State Hospital, I thought it might not be too bad, for I was still smugly congratulating myself upon having avoided prison. Sure, it was fenced and didn't really look like any resort hotel. But on the other hand, I saw no guards with machine guns in towers, so my stay might provide a nice, temporary change in my lifestyle. That's what I thought. However, I was disabused of this pleasant fantasy the moment I saw the inmates. Hooting, howling, hysterically obscene women squalled through the windows as attendants escorted me into one of the buildings.

There I was confronted by a woman who looked more like a man. Hard-jawed and hard-eyed, she had the feet, hands and personality of a storm trooper. Immediately she began to strip me to the skin, her hard, cold touch making me cringe.

Embarassed but defiant, I stood stark naked before her until she handed me a dismally ill-fitting grey-green nightgown. The fabric felt as hard and cold as the attendant's hands but I welcomed it to hide my body from her unnerving stare.

After that, I was locked into a cubicle with no furniture except a cot and with only one window, too high for me to see through. An animal in the zoo has more to console him than I had, for even a caged tiger can at least see freedom through the bars.

The building in which I was first lodged housed the violently insane and all newcomers to Rockland were held there until the degree of their violence could be determined.

During the tedious days I was locked in that tiny cell, my only distraction was to listen to the cries and moans of other patients.

I was a tough little fifteen year old but not tough enough to endure my first days at Rockland without fear. "This is definitely a madhouse," I thought. "Anyone who has to stay here long will go mad for sure."

I'd been committed for ninety days. I was allowed more freedom, but that still didn't make my life a picnic, for that freedom consisted of being allowed to join other patients in a shower where burly attendants washed us and spending days locked in a "day room" filled with assorted loonies.

Penned up in a room which smelled of human excrement, the inmates were noisy, silly, quarrelsome or apathetic. Some sat blank-eyed and slack-lipped, ignoring the saliva which threaded down their own chins. Some ranted and screeched. And some fought. These, no crazier that I was, were simply delinquents. . .herded into Rockland from the New York schools they'd terrorized.

I quickly identified with this set and was soon taking part in its wars. Fighting, as usual, was an outlet for my frustration. Fights vented my anger and added excitement to otherwise almost unbearable days. But they also added to my time in Rockland for,

with each infraction of the rules, my period of
commitment was lengthened.

The institution clearly felt that a girl so violent as I
had no place in polite Society.

During this difficult period, I was able to draw
comfort from two sources, both lesbian, but each
willing to show me some kindness.

One of the women who was good to me was an
attendant called Mama Crawford. She not only let
me out of a straight jacket during her shift but
occasionally brought me cokes and sometimes asked
me to help her wash the other patients.

In short, Mama Crawford treated me like a human
being instead of a wild animal. Further, she never
made any objectionable advances toward me;
although she was eventually fired because of her
lesbian affair with another inmate.

The other person who showed me kindness was a
woman in her thirties called Betty who expressed her
fondness through small caresses. And I hungered so
avidly for tenderness that I welcomed her overtures.

Even before coming to Rockland, I'd been so
dehumanized by the poverty and humiliation I'd
known that I was afraid I could no longer respond to
anybody's love. So, when Betty expressed her feel-
ings for me, I was pleased to discover that I could
react with affection.

No, I was not a lesbian. The masculinity of the
attendants nauseated me. Still, during my first stay at
Rockland, I learned why certain women love each
other for, when you've had to live without love, love
from any source becomes welcome.

However, I'd needed love so badly for so long that
the little bit I found at Rockland wasn't sufficient to
control my hostility. So I continued to get into
brawls. One of them was with an attendant who

caught me out of bed after the curfew hour and warned that once again my confinement at Rockland was going to be extended.

She was a crude, cruel woman who taunted me as she promised that my stay at Rockland would be prolonged every time I broke a rule. She seemed to take pleasure in the prospect, which filled me with a raging terror. The thought of being confined interminably in that place made me wild. The madness within its walls was driving me so mad that, faced with the gloating attendant, I finally lost all control.

Swinging wildly, I tried crashing my fist against a wall, pretending it was her hated face. But what I hit was a window, which shattered, ripping my arm and hand. I was so angry I didn't realize I'd hurt myself until I felt warm blood on my cold hand.

"Now you've done it," the attendant crowed. "You are going to pay for that."

If I could have pleaded innocent by reason of temporary insanity, I would have been cleared of all blame for what I did next, for I'd been goaded past the point of reason. Behaving purely out of instincts without a thought of the consequences, I lunged at the attendant and was saved from attacking her only when another attendant dragged me away to the infirmary.

There my cuts were bandaged, but that wasn't the only treatment I received. I was put in a cold-pack, a horror reserved for only the most violent patients.

A cold-pack treatment slows down bodily functions through a cooling process and theoretically calms a severely disturbed person. But I came out of the ordeal more disturbed than ever. I was stripped naked and bound in wet sheets on a bed of ice all night long in front of an open window.

As the winter wind blew over me, I was chilled in

more ways than one. Before that night I'd occasionally felt a spark of warmth toward a fellow human
being, but I came out of the cold pack as frozen
emotionally as I was physically.

During the hours of torture I sang Christmas carols
to keep myself conscious for I knew that, once
unconscious, I'd surely die. By singing, I rallied my
will to live, my will to stay alive long enough to get
even. I was determined to take revenge on the world
for what the world had done to me.

After the cold pack, I was put into a straight jacket.
But I was swaddled in more than restraining fabric
and leather. I was encased in a bitterness which made
me more hostile than ever.

While the stay at Rockland hadn't exactly eased
my craving for drugs, it had provided me with a new
source of supply—my psychiatrist. He was a kind,
sincere, good looking young man fresh from resi-
dency, and I thoroughly enjoyed putting him on with
stories I concocted about my past. He found me a
fascinating subject and called in consultants to help
diagnose my case. Further, as part of my treatment,
he prescribed "downers" which I was able to hoard
until I had enough to get stoned.

Nina, on the other hand, was so eager to get me off
drugs that she slipped me cokes mixed with scotch
because I'd told her I would leave drugs alone if only
I had something to ease my pain. Further, one
attendant gave me milk laced with booze. In addition,
I was able to get an occasional snort of heroin from
addicted patients whose friends smuggled their stuff
into the hospital. So Rockland, if anything, increased
my tendency toward addiction.

I stayed at Rockland for more than a year. Finally,
my psychiatrist said I was ready to re-enter the
world. "Oh, yes," I agreed. "I'm all straightened out.

49">49

I really and truly did want to make something of myself, and I did. Pretty soon I was both a mainliner and an unwed mother!

CHAPTER 8

Unwed Motherhood

When I finally got out of Rockland, I was a bigger mess than when I went in. I was still drinking and experimenting with drugs. I had suffered such serious psychological wounds that I had become de-humanized. And I'd completely lost interest in school.

To tell you the truth, I'd pretty much lost interest in learning when I realized I could never be a teacher. And after my stay in Rockland, the prospect of returning to a classroom was unbearable. How in the world could I, who'd been tied all night on a bed of ice, who'd spent her days with drooling, dreary maniacs under the care of muscular, mannish perverts, settle down under the discipline of a high school typing teacher?

By this time, most of the friends I'd had during my early Diamond deb days were drug addicts, unwed mothers, or both, and were now concerned more with staying alive than with education. I, following their example, also dropped out of school.

Nina had moved to the Bronx where she got a job in a Spanish-American restaurant which offered me a job serving drinks. Handing out beers certainly wasn't equal to teaching but, as jobs went, my new one offered certain opportunities. To drink!

Since I still had my senses, if not full humanity, I realized that I should get off drugs, and I looked upon my job in the bar as a possible cure. With ample liquor at hand, I reasoned that I could substitute booze for dope until I lost my craving for the latter.

Working in the bar wasn't hard and was actually rather pleasant, since I was naturally a night person and in such an alcohol-induced haze most of the time that I didn't worry about the dead-end nature of the job.

However, it failed to distract me totally from drug use, and it didn't give me as much money as I wanted and needed. So, in time, I progressed from merely joking and drinking with some of the men I met to going to bed with them.

With all I'd been through, it seemed that I was on a nightmare alley of no return. Because of my yearning for more money, I became what's known as a "housewife prostitute."

Needless to say, Nina and I weren't getting along very well by this time so I moved away from her and in with Betty, my lesbian friend from Rockland State Hospital. I had no more feeling for her than I did for the rest of Society but at least our association provided a roof over my head.

Nina couldn't understand that my heart was like rock; that my experiences with the opposite sex, beginning with what I'd endured from the janitor in the school basement and including rape when I was fifteen, had been such that men failed to stir me. I didn't especially dislike them. I just felt nothing at all for them except small gratitude that they were there to use whenever I prevailed upon one to buy me a drink.

The idea of a man taking me into his arms was neither attractive nor unattractive to me. But Nina couldn't understand this, for she'd grown up in a culture in which men and women played their clearly differentiated roles, where men were macho and women were provocatively acquiescent.

"It's true," I thought, "if I want emotional support and an expression of tenderness, I should find it with a fellow. A handsome fellow."

So subconsciously I began to scout around for a guy until I found one. The man for whom I settled wasn't exactly Clark Gable. Physically, he could be described as average.

But, wonder of wonders, he treated me as though I were the nice girl I'd once considered myself to be and, better yet, I was pleased when he touched me.

Happy to have found such a treasure, I never gave much thought to his background, assuming he was a reasonable clean-cut young man who, while he was no Prince Charming, was at least several cuts above the men I'd known in the past.

Gradually, as my emotional response to him increased, so did my physical response. I found it a pleasure to be held in his arms but an even greater pleasure in having myself reassured that a man could awaken my desires.

That's how it was until one night, in a burst of exchanged confidences, I told him what I'd been. When Angelo discovered I was a heroin user who'd been locked up in Rockland, he flew into rage. He was furious that I had deceived him so.

Yet it turned out that his past was even worse than mine for, while I'd been doing my stretch with crazies, he'd been doing a stretch with cons—Now that the truth was coming out, he admitted that he too was a heroin user who'd been in jail for offenses ranging from armed robbery to pushing drugs.

With our ugly histories out in the open, Angelo and I decided that we had a great deal in common—drab pasts spent in poverty, a hatred for the miseries of slum life, and a reliance on drugs for escape.

And we had another mutual interest to add to our shared interest in dope when I found that I was going to have our child.

Abortion never occurred to me, since it wasn't a part of the culture which produced me. Had it been, I probably wouldn't have existed myself. I felt about pregnancy the same way I felt about Angelo. I didn't particularly want either one, for I was growing rather tired of my lover by this time, but I didn't object to the embryo or the father sufficiently to want to get rid of either.

Motherhood, I reasoned, might even be good for me. New responsibility might force me into a better lifestyle..

So Angelo and I went to Nina and asked her consent to our marriage, something I had to have to get a license, since I was still only seventeen. But she emphatically refused it, arguing that it was better to live with Angelo without marriage if I didn't love him. And I agreed. Thus Angelo and I settled down to await the birth of a child.

Angelo, incidentally, had introduced me to more than pregnancy. Soon after I'd confessed to him that I was a heroin user, he'd shown me how to inject the drug into a muscle for a faster high. The sensation was a massive improvement over the one I'd gotten from snorting but it wasn't good enough. So next Angelo taught me how to inject heroin into the blood stream. Now I was a mainliner—a junkie.

After discovering I was pregnant, I had thought vaguely that my habit might be hurting the baby, but I didn't try to break it right away. During the fifth month of my pregnancy, however, reacting to a surprising surge of maternal instinct, I signed for a twenty-day cure which was being offered by the city of New York, consisting of the substitution of a synthetic narcotic for heroin.

The synthetic was an early form of methadone given to me daily in gradually decreasing amounts. Physiologically, the cure worked. My body was coming clean. But my mind wasn't. For, as a seventeen-year-old ex-gang deb with no marketable skills, carrying the child of a junkie whom I didn't love, I couldn't stand to face reality. I had to escape from my present and my future. And heroin was my out.

So after two weeks I left the drug cure program and surrendered to my increasingly expensive habit.

On the night of July 30, a typically steaming New York summer night, Angelo and I went into the streets to find some relief from the heat in our room which, needless to say, wasn't air-conditioned and, more importantly, to find some drugs.

The baby bulged within me, pressing uncomfortably against my stomach and my bladder. Perspiring and miserable, I hungered for the heroin which could guarantee relief from mental and bodily pain.

As oppressed as I was by the heat and the need for a fix, Angelo was irritable and, pretty soon, we were arguing about something. Today I honestly can't remember what it was we argued about. But the dispute grew more violent until I slapped him and he kicked me. He kicked me so hard that I fell to the pavement while the baby, undoubtedly wondering what his parents were up to, kicked me also.

I'm not sure whether Angelo's kick and my fall triggered my labor, but two hours later (two months before the baby was expected), I was at the hospital suffering the pain of contractions.

Nina was with me and so was Angelo who, if he wasn't remorseful for what he'd done, was at least interested in what might happen next.

Because I was very small and in poor physical condition, my labor was long and difficult and more excruciating than it would have been if I hadn't so badly needed a fix. By the time the baby was born, I'd been without heroin for thirteen hours so that I was being torn by withdrawal pains along with the usual labor pains.

The doctor in attendance had never seen me before and had absolutely no sympathy for drug addicts. So, when I began to scream and thrash about, he treated me by strapping me to the bed, cursing me all the while. For a bad moment there in the labor room, I thought I was back in Rockland State.

Finally, at 1:00 p.m. on July 31, my little boy was born—a three-pound drug addict who'd received his addiction as a birthday present from his junkie mother. Since he also had jaundice, his chances for survival were poor, and I'm sure my unsympathetic doctor must have thought, "With a mother like that, the kid will be lucky if he doesn't make it."

Nevertheless, the hospital staff, the doctor included, did everything possible to save the baby whose first earthly experience was to go through withdrawal. By contrast, while my tiny son was kicking the addiction I'd forced upon him, I wasn't kicking mine.

Because the stitches hurt, I was given a painkiller which killed more than one kind of pain. And on the evening of my son's birth I was high as a kite, flying on the medication the doctor had prescribed.

Motherhood wasn't so bad, I thought. While my

trip to the delivery room had given me a baby I could take or leave, it had also given me free fix of a sort. The white powder I'd taken was just what the doctor ordered—in more ways than one!

CHAPTER 9

Hooking to Support My Habit

I'd learned shoplifting before I'd learned English. Newly arrived in New York from Puerto Rico, Nina and I had scarcely settled in with my uncle and his family before my aunt took me out on a "boosting" expedition during which she filched assorted merchandise from assorted stores. I will say in her behalf that, in the slums of the city, shoplifting wasn't considered a crime so much as a necessary art employed by all who could master it.

And my aunt had mastered it well. She was a practiced booster, with techniques I copied until I too became a skilled shoplifter.

During one of my early outings, I was caught by a store detective but, since I was only a child, I was let off with only a reprimand, so I learned nothing from the experience except to be more careful next time.

After Dondi, my baby, was born, I relied for awhile on stealing to support my drug habit, if not my child. But shoplifting not only cost me my only good job I'd ever had, one in a department store, it failed to bring in enough money to pay for the dope I was using in ever-increasing quantity.

57

My habit was now costing $20 a day and growing. So, when my uncle came to me with a suggestion for making more money, I didn't reject the proposition out of hand.

Years earlier, my aunt had turned me into a shoplifter, and now my uncle was proposing that he turn me into an admitted, professional prostitute.

Working in the garment district, he knew all kinds of people (including representatives of organized crime) and, among his acquaintances was a man who'd pay me handsomely for just a few minutes of my time, he said. I could make $50 or $100 in no time at all, he went on to explain.

It wasn't as if my uncle was plotting the seduction of a virgin for he knew I'd already been selling myself, in a limited way, and he also knew I was a drug addict who needed money for dope. So why should I keep fooling around the way I'd been doing, he demanded, when I could make so much more money through serious prostitution?

Though I had hoped that having a baby would settle me into a better lifestyle, motherhood hadn't upgraded my morals or prospects in the least. Angelo and I were through with each other, and Nina had taken over the care of sickly little Dondi, since everyone—even I—knew that I wasn't fit to tend him.

When he was about a month old and finally released from the hospital to Nina's care, I'd once again felt a flicker of maternal instinct and had tried to nurse him. But the experiment was a failure which the visiting nurse advised me not to repeat. Though she didn't say that the best thing I could do for my baby would be to leave him strictly alone, that seemed so apparent that I began to take less and less interest in the tiny creature I'd so casually produced.

I craved my drugs more than I craved my son. My junk meant more to me than his welfare. Messed up by my habit, I was going to be a disgraceful mother at best, I reasoned, so why shouldn't I follow my uncle's suggestion and sell myself in a more business-like fashion at a much better rate of pay.

Thus I went to see the man in the garment district. Now my habit was costing more and more, with my moral standards declining and my need for drugs increasing. My body not only cried out for them, so did my mind, for during the moments when I had to face reality, I was sickened by what I had become.

Meanwhile, Nina had turned totally against me. And no wonder! Having loved me so much, my lifestyle caused her deep suffering. Still she didn't close her door to me until I showed her, in a shocking way, just how little I cared for her or for my baby.

One day, crazy for a fix, short of funds, and too sick to do much about it, I cleaned out Nina's apartment and sold almost everything she had. With the help of a cousin who had a truck, I hauled off all of her meager possessions except for one small bed and sold them to pay for junk.

Nina had worked tirelessly, endlessly, to pay for her small collection of necessities and comforts, but I didn't care. I wanted the $300 I sold them for much more than I wanted my grandmother to have a chair or a table or any of the other things she'd bought on time, with such difficulty.

Drugged though I was, I realized that Nina might not welcome me after I'd robbed her so I stayed away for awhile. Then when I saw her again, she told me I could stay away for good.

"You're a liar and a thief," she shouted. "Your friends are bums. Are you a junkie like they are?"

Until that moment, she'd refused to admit even to

herself that I was hooked on heroin. But now I rolled up my sleeves and showed her my "tracks."

"You get out," she ordered. "You stay away from us. We don't need junkies here."

So I'd reached the point where I no longer had Nina to comfort me, to remind me of my childhood when I'd vaguely wanted to be a nun, to insist that I was still a "good girl."

Instead, I had a madame for—yes—I was now working for a woman who booked a string of prostitutes.

It was a life I hated. I doubt that any woman enjoys it, for in the moments you're alone, your conscience confronts you, demanding "Why? Why are you doing this? It's so ugly!" Then, to escape your conscience, you turn to drugs. And, in order to buy your drugs, you must turn back to prostitution, to keep the vicious cycle going.

When my mind was fogged by drugs, I could work without thinking about what I was doing. Yet, because this madame refused to handle junkies, I couldn't let her know about my habit. So I always wore long sleeves to cover my needle marks.

Through the madame, I met a factory supervisor who liked for me to visit him at his office. I gave the madame ten percent of all that I earned this way but once, after I'd been to the factory, I decided to keep the entire fee.

I'd heard what could happen to a girl who tried to cheat her pimp or her madame, but greed outweighed my common sense and I kept all the money, thinking I could hide.

This was a foolish hope, however, because the madame employed guys to teach a lesson to any girl who deserved one. Therefore, I wasn't really surprised when one night, as I was working Prospect

Avenue, I saw one of these men, Louis, coming toward me.

All the terrible stories I'd heard about the punishment meted out to cheaters surged through my mind. I couldn't pray, since I didn't know how so, when I called on God, it was only to use His name as an expletive.

"Oh, God," I said, "he's going to kill me." And I almost hoped he would for, as I thought of the other possibilities, they seemed worse than death. He might slash me, cut my face to ribbons, so that everyone would know that I was a prostitute who'd cheated. For in my neighborhood a scarred face was often the badge of a dishonest hooker.

Worse, though, a slashing would leave me so ugly that I wouldn't be able to work. And the—oh, God!— then what would become of me?! If I couldn't work, how could I pay for my heroin? Altogether, I thought, death might be preferable to a slashing.

Louie, of course, had seen me and dragged me into a hallway. Holding me with one hand, he held an ugly knife in the other. Glaring at me, he must have remembered that he was the one who'd introduced me to the madame in the first place, so there was a special irony in his having been sent to punish me.

It was he who'd found me and said, "you don't have to work street corners to make money." And now he'd found me again and was going to fix it so I couldn't even hustle on a corner.

Okay, Louie," I told him, watching the blade all the while, "If you are going to do it, do it!

"Go ahead and cut me. Get it over with. I don't want to wait." I spoke with hatred, probably hating myself more than I hated Louie.

I can't explain what happened next except to say that God was protecting me. Because Louie gave me a shove, and then he walked away.

I was unscarred, free of him. He hadn't even scratched me.

Life on the streets often disfigures a girl physically as well as morally, but I survived prostitution with scarcely a physical blemish. I've been battered, and I've been cut but never on the face. A merciful God kept me whole, at least in a physical sense. At the time of my encounter with Louie, I thought it was blind luck that had saved me.

My life, though, was more difficult and dangerous after I left the madame, because no other madame would accept me as one of her girls. So I had to hustle in bars and at curb sides where there was no way of knowing how kinky a client might be. Girls who picked up men on the streets sometimes picked up sadists and killers. Also they were more visible targets for the vice squad which shortly busted me for the first time on a prostitution rap.

CHAPTER 10

I Cut a Cop

My first trip to jail was my worst—simply because I'd never been there before.

After Dondi's birth, which had generated a spark or two of mother love, my heart had reverted to stone. I cared for nothing except getting a fix.

Nothing, I thought, could thrill me or fill me with compassion or arouse any of the human emotions most girls experience. I was as totally de-humanized as a person could be. Or so I thought before my first visit to jail as a prostitute.

I'd just completed a business transaction with a trick in a room I frequented and was happy to have that phase of the evening behind me when two detectives, who'd been waiting outside the door, grabbed me.

"You're under arrest," one ordered.

The fellow who'd been with me literally turned pale. "I gotta go," he said, attempting to slide through. But a detective stopped him. "Police," the detective said. "Let's see your identification."

So nervous he could barely get his billfold out of his pocket, my client fumblingly produced his driver's license, all the while mumbling, "I didn't do anything. I haven't broken the law. I have to leave."

"You haven't broken the law, but you're going to testify against her," was the answer.

At that, the "john" nearly fainted. "I can't do that," he cried. If I do that, my wife will know...Hey, why don't you just let her go? Let's forget all about this."

The detectives exchanged tight, knowing grins. They'd seen this sort of thing happen before, over and over. "Uh-huh, buddy," one said, "If you don't testify, your wife is certainly going to know because we'll see that she does. So you'd better be ready to appear in court."

Meanwhile his partner was dragging me away toward my first visit to Prostitute Court.

During my years on the streets, I was to go to jail again and again for prostitution, for possession of narcotics and even for loitering, but I never got used to Prostitute Court, a place into which girls were herded like savage beasts by officers who would have had more respect for a pack of animals.

Before I went before the judge, I had to submit to a thorough physical examination, including a blood test conducted by a doctor and nurse who were obviously contemptuous of the human garbage they were forced to handle. As had been the case when I was bathed at Rockland, the hard, efficient, prying hands over my body made me cringe.

I'd hated doing what I'd done. I always hated letting men touch me for pay. And now I hated the touch of the doctor and nurse who handled me as impersonally as an automobile mechanic might handle a misbehaving engine.

"You're scum," the medical team's attitude

seemed to shout. "We hate to waste our precious skill on something like you."

While the examination was degrading, the court session was worse. Because it was in court that I had to listen to my trick testifying against me, in sordid detail.

I had to hear the detective describing what kind of person I was while the judge, digesting the information as impassively as a computer, looked at me as though I weren't alive.

And he was right, I thought, to look at me that way. For I was dead in every sense of the word but the physical.

Still in my teens, I had nothing to look forward to except more withdrawal pains, more days and nights of danger and despair, more trips to jail, more caresses from hot-handed men I loathed, and more loathing of myself, for there remained one emotion I could feel—self-hatred.

Though I became a repeater at Prostitute Court, I never learned to shrug away the casual cruelty of the place.

I could never hear a detective or a trick describe my activities with crude precision without inwardly flinching. And I could never accept the evident fact that high-priced call girls in mink coats were treated with more consideration than I. My treatment as compared to theirs emphasized the depths to which I'd sunk. We were all law breakers, they and I, but compared to them I was the dregs. Or so the attitude of court officials seemed to tell me.

The police had a particular dislike for me, or so I thought, because they were constantly hassling me. Now I believe that they gave me an unusually bad time because they knew I was young—very young— and they reasoned, "If we can make her life hard enough, maybe she'll give up hustling. A kid like this has no business on the streets."

Whatever their thoughts, they were after me all the time.

One afternoon, as I was standing only a block from precinct headquarters, an officer approached threateningly, ordering me to move on.

"But I'm not doing anything," I argued.

"You'd better get moving," he commanded, "or I'm going to run you in for loitering for purposes of prostitution."

"Hey, man," I fumed, "that's not what I'm doing. I'm just hanging around here. Look at all the people on this corner. Are you planning to arrest them all?"

The officer replied something insulting, provoking me to curse him and add a few comments about his background and personality. Even, perhaps, about his mother. Provoked even more than he'd provoked me, he reacted by hitting me and kicking me so hard that I fell.

Alarmed because he realized he'd gone too far, the officer bent over me. That was his mistake.

Now within arm's reach, his great, ugly (it seemed to me) face was within easy striking distance. My mind was so eaten away by drugs, I never thought of what the results might be as I drew my knife and slashed at his cheek.

Nor did I experience remorse at hurting a fellow human being, for I didn't feel human. The policeman was an alien being, the enemy, one who must be struck down and punished for the punishment I'd received from the world.

Fortunately, I neither killed the officer nor injured him seriously, but blood spurted from him, spattering bystanders as well as the two of us.

His fist crashed into me, his blood streaming over

us as we both growled like animals, attracting a crowd which quickly grew violent.

Habitues of that neighborhood cared no more for cops than I so they immediately rushed to my assistance. They, like I, were addicts with messed up minds and a real hatred for the police so that, while I was too badly hurt to keep much of a battle going, they were turning it into a small riot.

Meanwhile heavy feet were pounding toward us and heavy voices shouting. Fellow officers from the precinct house were arriving to come to the aid of the bleeding policeman.

Every inch of my body pulsed with pain. I was almost certain I'd received broken bones from the kicks and blows, yet I didn't surrender meekly to the police who grabbed me and dragged me into the station. To move at all filled me with wrenching pain but I kept trying to kick and claw my captors until finally they handcuffed me to a chair.

There I sat, sobbing out curses, shouting obscenities, and wishing that I could send every man in the precinct house to hell. By this time I must have looked like a demon from hell as, blood-spattered, bruised and filthy, I writhed against the ropes which now bound me to the chair.

All night I fought those bonds, for the officers refused to untie me, even when I asked to be released to go to the bathroom, and as a result, before morning, I reeked of urine as well as blood.

Finally they transferred me to the prison hospital where it was determined that my injuries included a fractured leg. As a matter of fact, I'd been so badly beaten that a couple of weeks passed before I was transferred to a cell.

Meanwhile I was charged with felonious assault against a police officer and advised by my court-appointed attorney that my best hope for getting out of jail within my lifetime would be to plead guilty.

"Enter a guilty plea," he had urged, "and you may get as little as twenty years with time off for good behavior. Otherwise, you'll do twenty-five years or more. I'm telling you, Cookie, cutting up a cop is serious."

I was being held on the floor with murderers, and the idea of spending a lifetime in such surroundings, with such company, appalled me. Besides, deprived of drugs, I was sick and frantic.

"Okay," I thought to myself, "maybe I'd better plead guilty and ask the court for mercy. If that policeman I cut testifies against me, I won't have a chance."

My victim was wearing a big patch on his cheek so that he looked more seriously injured than he really was, and I was terrified of the effect he'd have on a judge and jury. Still, I couldn't quite make up my mind to plead guilty until I got into more trouble by scalding a fellow inmate.

Among the women confined to the jail was a vicious customer named Tonga who took a special delight in picking on me. As she insulted and threatened me daily in the dining room, I was reminded of Norma, the big girl in junior high school whose taunts had indirectly launched me into gang life.

I was scared absolutely to death of Tonga, more afraid of her than I'd been of Norma, because I knew from her record that she was quite capable of killing.

But one day, as I sat down to a meal of hot soup, my hatred of her loomed so much larger than my fright that I grabbed up my bowl and threw its scalding contents all over her. Tonga squalled while guards overpowered me, which wasn't hard to do.

For, without more hot soup, I was disarmed.

I was hurried off to solitary confinement and reminded enroute that I was going to be charged with inciting a riot, as well as with assaulting a policeman.

My future couldn't have been more bleak! If I'd ever thought I could talk my way out of the first charge, I knew that, through that attack on Tonga. I'd lost my chance. True, I'd been afraid she might really kill me, but no judge would consider than an excuse for what I'd done.

"Okay," I reasoned with myself, "I'll just have to plead guilty—guilty to everything I've done. And I'll probably live and die in prison."

Strangely then, I thought of Dondi whom I seldom remembered. "When he's a grown man," I wondered, "will he come to see me?" Since I rarely went to see him, this seemed unlikely.

For quite a while nobody was allowed to see me in solitary, and during this period I decided definitely to plead guilty to any and all charges.

If I stayed in jail, Tonga or some other homicidal inmate might kill me, but if I got back to the streets I'd probably die anyway, I concluded.

I had no life, no future. So what did it matter how I pleaded? Had the means been available, I might have tried suicide again but I had no way to kill myself. I was at an all-time low when at last company came to my cell. It was my lawyer.

Surprisingly, he was all smiles, and I wondered why, because I could think of nothing about my case that should make him happy.

"Cookie," he beamed, getting right to the point, "you're practically out of here."

"Hey, man, what are you saying?" I thought he

had to be joking unless I'd gone totally mad and was imagining the entire scene.

"I mean it," he assured me. "When you were brought in, the police doctors took pictures of your injuries which show that you'd been so badly beaten that the department wants to drop the case."

"You're one lucky girl. I thought you'd be in jail for the rest of your life, but instead the City of New York wants you out in a hurry, because it doesn't want a jury to know what six big cops did to one eighty-pound teenage girl. In fact, the city's afraid you'll sue."

"Cookie, you'd better believe that Somebody Up There is taking care of you."

Surely God must have intervened when those charges were dropped, but I never thought about that. All I could think of was getting back to my drug supply which I hoped would make life partially bearable.

Yet on the streets life was as miserable as it had been in jail and certainly a lot more dangerous.

CHAPTER 11

The Law of the Jungle

As a junkie-prostitute, I walked in the shadow of death which often reached out a clammy hand to claim me.

I could have died in a dozen different ways, perhaps at the hand of a sadistic "john," a drug-crazy fellow junkie, or by my own hand. For I attempted suicide more than once, while more than once I almost died from an accidental overdose. Further, I occasionally invited death by ripping off some tough customer who might have turned on me. And once I went so far as to mug a dope dealer!

This bit of bravado was the ultimate of insanity. It happened on one of the nights when I was literally aching for a fix. Because I hated prostitution—really hated it—I always waited until the last possible minute to go out into the streets. And by that time, I was usually suffering the first symptoms of withdrawal.

Anyway, that's how it was on the night I foolhardily ripped off a dealer. I was too sick to stand on a corner and solicit, though I knew that's what I would

71

have to do if I were to get money for a fix. So I was standing inside the doorway of a building, in the entry way, leaning against an old steam radiator that spit and sputtered while it failed to warm me.

The walls of the entry were dirty, streaked with stains that looked and smelled like dried mustard. The stair railing, extending up and up to some distant hell in which people were quarreling, was dusty and sticky to the touch. So that altogether the building seemed as near dead as I, a fitting environment for a retching, shivering, pain-filled, mainlining hooker.

I was clinging to the radiator, listening to it gasp out its little spurts of steam, when a killer named Chino walked in. As killers went, he was rather debonnaire, graced with a sporty, little goatee which made him look like Satan himself. He was also big and bad and so vicious that he's doing time right now for murder—

Chino was my kind of guy, the kind I usually hung around with, because I was so small I needed some protection. My weakness seemed to bring out whatever gallantry was left in the biggest, toughest, nastiest street prowlers so they'd protect me from others who were as mean as they.

Chino studied me critically. "Hey, Cookie," he said, "I don't like to see you sick this way."

His interest in me wasn't at all romantic, but it was genuine, because he felt a kinship for me born out of our shared degradation. I was his sister of a sort, a sister in poverty, a sister in filth, a sister in hopelessness.

"Look," Chino continued in as kind a tone as ever used to anybody, "I know that you don't feel like going out on the street and working tonight, so here's what I think you should do:

"There's a dope dealer up on the corner who's

loaded with money and drugs. He's got plenty. So let's go up there right now and rip him off."

The close call I'd had with Louie after cheating the madame should have taught me not to invite the hatred of hard core criminals and, if I'd had any sense at all, I would have told Chino "no." For to mug a dealer was equivalent to asking for horrible revenge. After doing a thing like that, to be killed would be to get lucky. The pains of cold turkey withdrawal would be nothing compared to the pains I could expect at the hands of a ripped-off dealer and his source.

Yet I was so addled by illness and my need for a fix that I said, "Sure. Yeah, Chino, let's go."

So we went up to the guy and pulled him into a hallway where Chino drew a gun and handed it to me. "Hold this on him, Cookie," Chino instructed, "while I search him." With the .45 in my hand, I felt like Wonder Woman—all powerful, indestructible and completely unconcerned that I was courting death.

The dealer was coldly, deadly furious, because he was not only losing his money and his merchandise but he was going to have to explain to his boss that a ninety-pound girl had held him at gunpoint while he was being robbed.

"I'm going to get you for this," he promised, his eyes holding me like a cobra's holds a bird just before he strikes. "You won't be able to hide from me, and I won't forget."

I knew he wasn't lying. Yet, even in the face of his threat, Chino and I had no thought of retreating from our suicidal venture. "Just keep the gun on him," my colleague instructed as he rummaged through our victim's pockets, his shoes, and every conceivable hiding place in his clothing and on his body.

"I think I've got it all," he finally said. But I wasn't satisfied.

"You hold the gun while I search," I told him greedily.

And then, doing the most senseless thing I'd ever done in my life, I not only searched the dealer but I cursed and slapped him. It was as though all the anger pent up within me were being exorcised—all the anger I'd ever felt against the classmates who'd shunned me, the guy who'd raped me at fifteen, the cruelties I'd suffered at Rockland and in jail, the thousands of days I'd lived in bleak, futureless poverty.

All of this was behind every blow I struck. I wanted to hurt somebody as badly as I'd been hurt. . .worse than I'd been hurt. So I slapped the dealer again and again.

Finally, convinced that we really did have all of his drugs and money, we let him go and then, but only then, did I fully realize what the repercussion would be. "I'm going to get you," had been the dealer's last threat, directed specifically at me because even he was a little afraid of Chino. "You're going to be awfully sorry for what you've done."

"Hey, Chino," I cried, "I've got to get out of here. I've got to get lost."

And that's what I did. I lost myself in a new neighborhood into which, amazingly, the dealer and his friends didn't follow.

I did meet that dealer one more time, much later, and under different circumstances I could never have envisioned. But this isn't the time to tell about that. The meeting comes further along in my story.

Meanwhile, I continued to invite death in other ways, all of which grew out of my habit and profession. A girl who works the streets can't expect to attract the highest type of clientele and, as I've mentioned earlier, I once wound up with a stab-happy maniac. However, he wasn't the only sadist I encountered.

On another occasion when I achingly needed drugs, I stupidly climbed into a long, white automobile with a man who took me into strange territory where I was brutally handled by seven men who beat me and knocked out my tooth. They never tried to kill me but I thought they might do it accidentally. Yet they didn't frighten me as badly as a fellow junkie did after I had agreed to do him a favor.

I wasn't keen about doing a favor for Teddy because he'd never done one for me, or for anyone else for that matter. While there actually is some honor among junkies, a willingness to help each other in a crisis, there wasn't a shred of honor in Teddy's makeup. He was the kind who'd steal drugs from a so-called friend, or money, or anything else he wanted.

So I wasn't so eager to please when he asked, "Cookie, would you get my works for me? There are cops all over the neighborhood who might search me, but they won't search a woman.

"So come on, Cookie. Get 'em for me, will you?"

He was telling the truth when he said the police wouldn't search a woman, because a male officer wasn't allowed to search a female suspect. Only a police woman could do that. So it wasn't unusual for a girl to carry a guy's syringe, cooker, etc. for him.

Still I started to jerk away from Teddy because I, too, needed a fix so badly that I was beginning to double up with pain.

"Not now," I told him. "I'm sick, man."

"Come on, Cookie," he begged—no—ordered. For he was holding my arm so tightly that it hurt as he shoved me toward the entrance of the building. My works are right in the hall under the radiator," he said. "So get them for me."

"Oh, all right, Teddy," I answered, eager to be rid of him so that I could try to find a fix for myself.

He followed me to the building where I found his works and handed them to him, thinking that his cooker and syringe were all that he wanted. But he wouldn't let me go. Still holding onto me, Teddy ordered, "Let's go upstairs."

"No," I cried. "Let me go. I need a fix. I'm sick. I got your works for you, so leave me alone."

"Get on up those stairs," he snarled, yanking and shoving me along.

"What's the matter with you?" I wanted to know. "Hey, look man, I'm too sick to climb up there."

But climb I did, my legs almost buckling beneath me, until we reached the roof where Teddy whirled me around to face him and then struck me in the mouth so hard that I collapsed.

For four hours he tormented me sexually and in other ways, sometimes threatening to throw me off the roof. While my stomach knotted with withdrawal pains, he raped me, and then I was almost sure he'd pitch me over the parapet knowing that, if I lived to tell other addicts that he'd abused me while I needed a fix, they'd kill him.

"Come on, Teddy," I begged finally. "Get it over with. Kill me." He struck me again.

"Kill me now if you're going to do it." I didn't say this out of bravery but because I was so tired of being tortured. "I'm too weak to fight you," I said, "so just hurry up and throw me off the building and get it over with." He was holding me so near the roof's edge that I really believed he was going to pitch me to my death right then and there.

But instead of shoving me over the brink, he pulled me back and, after slapping me a time or two, let me go.

Like the drug dealer I mugged, Teddy re-entered my life again at a much later date under amazing conditions which I'll describe at the proper time.

Because of the lifestyle I followed and the kinds of men with whom I consorted, only a series of miracles kept me alive. And a miracle saved me once more when, by minutes if not by seconds, I escaped murder and dismemberment.

Through nothing less than a miracle, I avoided a man who killed another hooker in a horrible way and who's never been caught.

CHAPTER 12

Too Unlucky to Die

Expensive call girls whose business appointments are made through well-established madames escape many of the hazards of the world's oldest profession. Their clients are carefully screened before girls are made available to them, to insure that each man is willing and able to pay for the goods he's ordered and that he's free from peccadillos which might permanently damage the merchandise.

But a girl on the streets has no protection, especially if she works free-lance, without a pimp.

Most men who pick up girls on corners are harmless, just lonely fellows who want companionship for an hour. Some are traveling men who have to be away from their wives for long periods. Some are older men who have trouble making social contacts with girls. Some men will pay girls just to talk with them, they are so desperate for companionship.

There was a Portuguese sailor who paid $50 for only a few minutes of a girl's time and didn't even want sexual relations. He touched her but that was all. He was a strange one, all right.

Some of the men are single and good looking and

could undoubtedly have a woman without paying her, but for some reason they find prostitutes exciting.

These were the odd but harmless johns a girl could pick up on the streets. However, there was always the danger that she'd pick up a man who hated women or sex or simply hated prostitutes and only wanted a chance to abuse them.

Or even kill one. Criminologists believe Jack the Ripper was like that.

After I'd cheated the madame and lost her protection, I was safe enough for awhile, because of a woman named LaNegra and a bartender named Mike.

LaNegra was well known in the neighborhood, an experienced and, in a peculiar sense of the word, a "respected" prostitute, who took an interest in me. She gave me advice and kept an eye on me the way that a master carpenter supervises a young apprentice. It was from LaNegra that I truly learned (and no pun is intended here) the tricks of my trade.

As for Mike, he let me work out of his bar for awhile and, although this didn't mean that I was under his protection, it gave me a certain status and security.

I'd go there every night from seven until midnight to drink with his customers who'd then become my tricks.

I never drank hard liquor, only creme de cocoa, so I never became a troublesome drunk.

One night, though, I became a troublesome junkie, because I'd started barbituates as well as heroin, and when you mix the two, you get nasty. I started cursing and screaming, threatening to cut someone, until Mike, who was trying to run a relatively classy place, had to throw me out. I remember that he was actually sorry to have to do it because he knew how young I was and what a rough life I'd lead hustling on the corners but, since he had to make a choice between what was good for his business and what was good for me, he kicked me out and told me to stay gone. He was a hard man, but he had a heart.

Anyway, after Mike's bar was barred to me, I was on my own with a drug habit which was getting progressively worse and with no one except God to look after me.

As it turned out, God did an excellent job of shielding me from everybody except myself, though I never gave Him credit for it. When I escaped a long prison sentence, when I escaped Teddy, when I survived overdoses and other horrors, I simply congratulated myself upon having been lucky each time. I didn't even fall to my knees in prayer after Rosa, another prostitute, was killed in my place, which sounds unbelievably dramatic, but that's what happened.

Rosa was an old-timer called LePiojosa which means "lice" for very good reason. She looked shopworn and dirty so that, if a man had a choice of girls, she'd be one of the last he'd take.

We were standing on a street corner this particular morning, talking with each other and looking for business when, on sudden impulse, I decided to get something to eat. Telling Rosa goodbye, I started walking away and saw her climb into a light green sedan.

Momentarily I thought, "If I'd been there, he would have taken me, for I'm much cleaner and younger than she is." And that thought was to return again and again when, a short time later, Rosa's dismembered body was found in Central Park.

Her last trick was a maniac who's never been

caught. And he would've been my last trick had that impulse not taken me off the corner in the nick of time.

A couple of times I had almost died from an overdose and, on one of those occasions, I was actually pronounced dead and would have been sent to the morgue except for my grandmother who was determined that I stay alive, though I didn't really want to.

That time I'd been discovered unconscious and rushed to the hospital where I was declared DOA (dead on arrival.) But my grandmother, summoned to the scene, wouldn't accept that I was gone.

The medical staff, believing that I was past human help, had turned its back on me as it would on any corpse, while Nina continued to scream and plead, "Help her; she's not dead. Help her!"

A doctor, moved by compassion for a heartbroken grandmother if not for a junkie, tried to console her. "There's nothing more we can do," he assured her. "Your granddaughter is gone."

But as Nina kept on howling and weeping, insisting that he do something, he wearily turned back to my still, ashen body. "See, she's not breathing," he confirmed. Then his hand touched my foot and he became instantly attentive.

"Hey," he called to a nurse, "maybe this girl isn't dead after all. Her foot is warm. Let's try to save her."

I'd taken my near-fatal fix eight hours earlier and should have been in hell by this time but instead, thanks to the intensive efforts of a medical team now working furiously, I was on my way back to life.

Three days later, I opened my eyes to become aware of my surroundings. At the same time, I became aware that I needed a fix so, although I was still listed as in serious condition and almost too weak and dizzy to stand, I struggled out of the hospital.

"If I could just get a fix," I thought, "I'd be okay." Or if I could just die, things would be even better.

Another overdose which was almost lethal put me not only into a hospital but into jail.

I was still in my teens at the time and had been living with an elderly Jewish man who actually thought he was in love with me. So he'd rented a little room for me in a boarding house where he thought I would be safer and happier.

One day, though, I went into the bathroom, locked the door and took an overdose. If I'd had a private bath, I guess I would have died. But since the landlady and everybody else in the building shared the facility, the locked door attracted attention.

People knocked and knocked and knocked on the door and finally, getting no response, broke the catch. There they found me, on the floor, with the needle, syringe and cooker, more dead than alive.

The landlady didn't call for a priest but for a cop who told me, after I came to several hours later, "You're busted for possession of narcotics." Nobody cried, "We're glad you're alive." The police only commented, "You're going to do some time."

And I did. Ninety days of it.

CHAPTER 13

Crazy Cookie Is Deported

For a miserable period of my life, if I wasn't in jail, I was in a mental institution—or so it seemed.

As far as jail was concerned, I was in so often that I adjusted to doing time. I was institutionalized so much that I could have done a year blindfolded and it wouldn't have bothered me much. I became a "regular" who was accepted and even respected by other inmates. I even developed a sort of respect for the officers at the jail, even though I still hated them.

But, despite this hatred, I didn't give trouble, because I knew that, if I did, five days would be added to each month of my sentence.

As for my time in mental institutions—Bellevue and Rockland—some of that was spent voluntarily and some against my will.

Life is always hard for a junkie, especially a woman junkie, but during drug famines, when heroin isn't available at any price, it becomes deadly. Neighborhoods frequented by addicts grow acrid with the vomit of drug users who foul the streets as they go through withdrawal. Girls are murdered by almost subhuman sufferers, insane for fixes.

The devil himself could scarcely design a hell more appalling than certain New York streets during periods of drug shortage. And during such periods Rockland became suddenly popular as junkies checked themselves in for ninety-day cures.

I checked in a number of times to receive short-term therapy which left me physically clean but psychologically as addicted as ever. Because, even after my body had lost its hunger for heroin, my mind craved the forgetfulness available through drugs.

I couldn't bear to remember all that I'd done, nor to contemplate my bleak, hopeless future. I couldn't stand life without dope. So, as quickly as I was released from Rockland, I headed back to the streets in search of drugs.

Still, my trips to the hospital (as well as to jail) probably saved my life because, without withdrawing from drugs occasionally, the average junkie dies in a year or two from disease, an impure supply, or malnutrition.

Once, when I was at Rockland, a female psychiatrist gave me a pep-talk which was temporarily more effective than any of the other help I'd received.

"You've got the will power to give up drugs," she said. "I know you do. You've kicked drugs in jail when you had no other choice, but you can do it on your own with nobody making you do it except yourself. I know that you can. You're too smart to die on the streets.

"Cookie, you're a bright girl who can save herself. Use your willpower and you can kick your habit for good."

"You mean I should kick with drugs right out there on the street?" I wanted to know.

"That's what I mean," the psychiatrist said. "If you kick when nobody's forcing you to do it, you'll be cured. You'll never have to sell yourself again to pay for a fix. Just think about that."

Well, thinking about that, I decided to put my willpower to work and come clean for good. If the psychiatrist felt I could do it, maybe I could. If it meant escape from prostitution forever, I'd follow her enthusiastic advice.

Nina wasn't so sure that I had all the willpower the psychiatrist had been talking about, but she agreed to let me go through withdrawal at her place. And, with no one except myself to offer courage, I made it!

For three days I wretched and cried and endured the sheer agony of kicking cold turkey. Even though I knew that, at any moment, I could have walked (wobbled really, since I was so weak) out the door and straight to a drug source.

As my suffering began to abate, it was replaced by self-pride I hadn't known in years. I was doing it! I was overcoming my hellish habit through willpower stronger than my condition. I was a special person after all, or so I gloriously believed for the first time since I'd been raped and dropped from my academic high school classes.

"Cookie," I told myself, "you're terrific." And others told me so, too, when at last I walked out of the borrowed room—thin and weak, but smiling. I'd cleaned myself up outwardly as well as inwardly to greet astonished neighbors who knew what I'd done and were almost as proud of me as I was of myself.

Nina was happier than I was, if possible, as she patted me and wept, "I've prayed for this so long."

And even Dondi, who scarcely knew this emaciated creature who was his mother, permitted me to fondle him briefly before escaping to the great-grandmother who was rearing him.

Relatives came around to congratulate me, though

in a manner which subtly said they didn't have much faith in my redemption. And their doubt infuriated me.

After my bold display of willpower, how could they question my total cure? Yet smiles partially hidden by coughs, exchanged glances, revealing tones of voice, told me that relatives and friends were accepting the new Cookie with reservations.

Finally, the atmosphere in the apartment became so burdensome that I had to escape. "Where are you going?" Nina asked suspiciously for, yes, even Nina was less than totally convinced that I was permanently clean.

"I'm going out for some air," I said.

"Don't go," Nina begged. "You're not ready. If you go, they'll sell you dope."

So now the suspicion was out in the open! I still wasn't to be trusted! I was still a freak who needed a keeper.

I surged with rebellious rage. "These people are driving me crazy," I snapped. "I'm cured. I quit cold turkey, didn't I? Nobody made me. So I know what I'm doing." And, with that, I lit out for my favorite neighborhood bar.

I didn't go there for a fix, only to calm down. But when I saw the well-known faces of junkie friends, when I heard their "Hey, welcome back," I knew I was back where I'd probably end my days—among the sick, addicted victims of the drug scene. For I was still one myself. Despite my stalwart, three-day performance at Nina's, I was a junkie too.

Within two hours, I'd shot heroin into my vein and was flying. So much for the psychiatrist at Rockland! So much for the willpower!

As I took more and more drugs, I progressed from temporarily rattled to completely mad. After a drug panic during which I was doing what we call "the bombitas," I began to see visions and hear voices. Bombitas can be compared to amphetamines in liquid form, which I took by injection, and I'd shot quite a lot of it before I really began to feel insane.

Voices shouted at me; monsters chased me; and I saw policemen everywhere—even in baby carriages. Once, as I was headed for Rockland, I warned the cabdriver that assassins were out to get me. I thought they were surrounding the taxi and that both the cabbie and I were doomed.

My warning must have inspired the driver to deliver me to the state hospital in record time.

I was warning other addicts, too, that someone was after us. "That's the man," I'd yell, "Watch him; watch him." Whereupon my fellow mainliners would try to get away from me. "You're gonna get us busted," they'd say. "Get away from us; you're crazy."

Appropriately, they called me Crazy Cookie, especially after I began sticking straightpins through my cheeks, inviting and getting some serious infections. Even though, in moments of rationality, I though I'd be disfigured for the rest of my life, I never asked a doctor to treat these sores.

Addicts, witnessing my festering exterior, got an inward look at themselves, and they ran when they saw me coming. While I was in this state I had a horrifying experience which, to this good day, I can't classify as real or imagined.

I'd gone out to turn a trick and came back screaming, "I had to stab him; I had to stab him!" Voices had warned me that the man I was with was going to hurt me as men had hurt me before. And in my addled mind, I was sure I had stabbed him. Had I?

I'll never know. A couple of drug addicts slapped

their hands over my mouth, whispering fiercely, "Shut up. You're gonna get yourself busted. Shut up!" Wrenching away from them, I ran screaming toward Nina's which was about a mile away.

Voices continued to harangue me, not voices of the concerned drug addicts but imaginary voices driving me to run faster and faster. Finally I was able to throw myself into Nina's apartment and slam the door, but the threatening voices followed.

"Come out," they yelled. "We want you. Come out." Imaginary fiends beat on the door as they wailed for me to surrender to them.

Terrified, I grabbed a butcher knife to defend myself and hurried to the fire escape. But there was no escape from the voices. "We want you," they kept calling.

Meanwhile Nina, with a very real voice, was crying and screaming. I was frightening her as much as the voices were frightening me.

As I stood quivering, butcher knife ready, she called my uncle who hurried over to help her. Somehow they managed to get me into a cab and deliver me to Rockland State where I arrived a wild, totally disoriented creature.

I'd gone there first as a miserably unhappy child with a keen mind and a bruised but still viable desire to do something worthwhile with my life. Now, only a few years later, I was returning, a mainlining madwoman, dangerous to herself and to others.

The best thing that could happen to me would be for me to die early, for if I managed to survive my suicidal lifestyle, I'd probably have to exist behind bars. Prison bars or, more likely, asylum bars.

"You've cooked your brain for good," my uncle declared, with some degree of satisfaction. "This time they're going to lock you up for good."

Well, that time they didn't. They put me in the violent ward, Ward 21, but within a couple of months after my mind had cleared a little, I was able to work an angle that set me free for a brief period.

During a visit to my psychiatrist, I put on an act that was worthy of an Oscar. Exuding mother love like the Sistine Madonna, I begged, "When can I see my baby? How long does a mother have to wait before she can see her little boy?"

My performance was so convincing that the doctor called Nina and asked her to bring Dondi in for a Sunday visit.

The day that they came was so beautiful that I was allowed to take Dondi for a walk on the hospital grounds while Nina conferred with the psychiatrist. But I didn't restrict my stroll to hospital property.

Instead, leading my baby, I walked away and took a bus to the city. When our absence was discovered, a thirteen-state alarm went out because, though I was Dondi's mother, I wasn't his legal guardian, so I was wanted for kidnapping.

However, I didn't hold my "kidnap" victim for long. Realizing that, if Dondi were returned to Nina, the authorities would be less interested in finding me, I dropped him off in the lobby of an aunt's apartment building and then phoned the aunt to tell her where he was.

Everything had worked out just fine, I told myself.

Good ole dumb Nina had been my patsy once again. She'd brought me my child who became my ticket to freedom.

Good ole Nina wasn't quite so dumb as I imagined, though. When I went by to see her a few months later, she turned me over to the police who immediately turned me over to Rockland, where I was thrown into the "Snake pit," Building 60, the residence of the hopelessly insane.

During previous visits to the hospital, I'd become so sly that I'd once managed to escape by jamming a doorlock with chewing gum as I went out for my recreation period. But now there was no way out. Snake Pit inmates were usually there for life!

The windows were so high I couldn't see out. Visitors were limited to one every two or three months.

One day a fellow patient fell dead right in front of me and her death seemed to confirm my awful fear that I, too, was going to die behind bars.

Finally, after I'd been in the Snake Pit for a year, Nina, proving she was still good, if not dumb, came to see me. At the sight of her disgraceful granddaughter, she began to sob. "Don't worry," she promised. "I'll get you a lawyer and try to get you out."

She did both. She hired a lawyer and through him was able to rescue me from what had promised to be endless confinement. He urged the hospital to release me and let me be deported to Puerto Rico, arguing that my departure would save the New York taxpayers money.

The state agreed to the bargain, only if I would wait two years before I could come back to the mainland, so I was carted to the airport and shipped out.

Amazing as it may seem, Nina had let me take Dondi along to Puerto Rico, in hopes that my maternal instincts and the responsibility of caring for him would keep me out of further trouble.

But I didn't have the responsibility long. Two weeks after my flight to Puerto Rico, I was flying back to New York. I entered under an assumed name. Naturally I headed back to Nina where I turned Dondi over to my grandmother before hitting the streets again in search of drugs.

CHAPTER 14

Looking For a Cure

Since nobody else had been able to cure me of my drug habit—neither psychiatrists, policemen or even myself (on the occasion when I'd voluntarily kicked cold turkey)—I turned to my father for help.

Yes, to my father, dead by his own hand at seventeen!

Although most Puerto Ricans are technically Catholic, they generally put their basic faith in spiritualism. So as a child in my native village, I'd attended many seance-like meetings called veladas, presided over by my aunt who was a medium and the man next door who was "president of the table." I didn't really believe in spiritualism, anymore than I believed in Catholicism, yet I couldn't completely deny the power of either.

Maybe, I thought, there actually was a God, though He didn't seem to care much about me. If there was a God in Heaven, he seemed to be ignoring Cookie in her earthly hell. Or that's how I, a religious illiterate, had analyzed the situation.

On the other hand, I reasoned, it was possible that the spirits of the dead were keeping a collective eye on me and affecting my miserable life. For as a child, at spiritual meetings, I'd been told that angry spirits from beyond the grave were responsible for our misfortunes. Maybe, I thought, there was something to this.

So I decided to consult a spiritualist. Actually it was a group of spiritualists, who suggested that I swallow and bathe in various foul-smelling concoctions. This didn't appeal to me in the least. Yet I couldn't reject one of their ideas.

Because my father had committed suicide, they said, his spirit was restless and could only find peace with my help. This restless spirit had placed a curse on me in order to get my attention, the spiritualists explained.

Therefore, they suggested that I should attend a series of veladas in an effort to confront my father's ghost so that he could tell me what it was he wanted me to do for him and so that I could ask him to release me from the curse.

Well, I didn't believe this completely but neither did I entirely disbelieve it. So I began attending the velada. I was attending, but my father wasn't.

Finally, however, his fretful, wandering spirit seemed to manifest itself. For one night, immediately after the velada began, the president of the table, in a trance-like state, seized me by the throat and began to choke me with supernatural strength.

Could he be acting as proxy for my father's ghost?

That was the opinion of the group and, if they were correct, the ghost was homicidal, because I was nearly choked to death before several men were able to tear the president away from me.

I still was not convinced that my father's spirit had put a curse on me or had attacked me but, if it had, I wanted no more to do with it. I decided that communicating with stray souls was dangerous business which I should avoid in the future. So I went to no more veladas.

Spiritualism, I concluded, would never cure my habit. I would have had better luck with another unorthodox method of treating drug addiction, had I given the method a chance.

But I ran away from my first opportunity to be healed by corporate prayer.

One day, burning as usual with a craving for drugs, I ran into a church with the intention of conning the priest out of enough money to pay for a fix. A priest, I expected, would be both kind and simple-minded enough to fall for the line I was about to give him. I'd already proved myself a good actress on several occasions, in courtrooms and at Rockland, so I felt sure I could convince a priest that I was a sweet, starving girl who needed money for food.

"Father," I began, exhibiting what I hoped was a desperate but winning smile, "Please help me. I'm so hungry I can't remember when I've eaten last. Please let me have enough money for at least one good meal.

"Please. If you don't, I'll die."

The priest studied me carefully. He'd seen plenty of drug addicts in his time and wasn't fooled a minute. But he did manage to fool me.

He didn't promise to give me money but his manner was so compassionate that I felt sure he was going to, so I didn't run away.

"Come into my office and visit with me for awhile. There's someone I want you to meet, someone who will help you."

"This is going to be okay," I thought. "He believes me, so I'll wait awhile. Though I hope I don't have to wait too long for the sucker who's going to bring me money."

The priest made a phone call while I fidgeted and hoped I wouldn't go into withdrawal until the price of my next fix arrived.

"Who's coming?" I wondered, as I answered the Father's questions about my life with what I assumed were convincing lies.

Finally, a young man arrived who was introduced as Nicky Cruz. He was short and tough-looking—not at all what I'd expected. Nicky got right to the point.

"You're a drug addict," he announced, "and what you need isn't a fix but a cure."

"That's what you're going to get, because I'm going to take you to a place where you can be freed from your habit."

You may have read Dave Wilkerson's book, *The Cross and the Switchblade*, or Nicky's book, *Run, Baby, Run*, in which case you're familiar with Nicky's history. He was a gang warlord, as deadly as a cobra. He probably would have wound up on Death Row or dead, had not a young preacher from Pennsylvania named Dave Wilkerson reached him with the truth that Jesus loved him.

Nicky was a hard-sell; when he finally accepted Christ's mercy and asked the Lord to take over his life, he literally became a new creature, just as the Bible promises each of us can become, through Jesus.

Nicky began to work with Dave in a mission program call Teenage Evangelism (later named Teen Challenge) and it was as a representative of missionary effort that he'd come from Brooklyn to the Bronx to try to redeem a girl junkie.

I could have refused to go with Nicky and he wouldn't have kidnapped me, but evidently the Lord was prodding me in the right direction, because I sullenly put myself into his hands. "Okay, man," I said, "let's go to this place you're talking about."

Nicky took me back to Brooklyn and to the third floor of an old house where I was welcomed at the door by smiling people who told me God loved me and would see me through the ordeal of becoming permanently clean.

"You're going to kick right up here," Nicky said as he ushered me into the third floor room, "but it isn't going to be so bad this time, because I'm going to be with you, praying for you. And the Lord's going to be with both of us."

As good as his word, Nicky stayed right with me, encouraging me, praying for me, and I went through withdrawal within a day, with less discomfort than usual. Even I would have to admit that the Lord heard and answered prayers—or Nicky's prayers anyway—but I still doubted that He would hear mine.

With Nicky Cruz beside me, beseeching the Lord, a miracle could happen and, if Nicky had been able to stay beside me for a longer time, I might have stayed with Teenage Evangelism until I was permanently released from drugs. However, Nicky couldn't give all his time and attention to me, and when he had to go away for a few days, I went away too.

I split from the house in Brooklyn and headed for the streets where I knew I'd find the miracle I was used to—the miraculous escape from reality which came with drugs.

Prayer was all right for Nicky, I thought. It worked for him. But a fix was the thing that worked for me, so I headed out to find one.

CHAPTER 15

The Healing Begins

On the streets, I was living on borrowed time. There were so many ways to die that I was fast exhausting the short life-span allotted to a prostitute junkie. So I think I can factually say that One-Eye Dutch saved both my life and my soul when he dragged me back into Dave Wilkerson's sphere of influence.

One-Eye Dutch was a black man who'd earned his descriptive name when he'd tried to mug a man armed with a metal-tipped umbrella. A junkie criminal at the time, in recent months he had changed. No longer mean and strung out, he prowled the New York slums performing kindnesses like the Good Samaritan and talking about Jesus.

No one, at this point, could be more in need of help than I, so Dutch zeroed in on me with a fervor that couldn't be defeated. He talked endlessly of how much Christ loved me and how He could change my life. But even though I remembered vaguely that Nicky Cruz had said the same thing while offering himself as living proof of the redemptive power of Jesus, I wasn't impressed.

"Leave me alone, man," I told Dutch. "Can't you see I don't want you hanging around with all your crazy talk?"

But Dutch refused to give up and finally, when he found me sleeping on the sidewalk one night, cold and sick, he covered me with his coat, and I began to take his message seriously.

Something or somebody had obviously changed him, so maybe he really knew of a secret source that could change me. Anyway, I could no longer commit myself to Rockland voluntarily and I needed some place to dry out one more time. So I decided I might as well give Dutch and his mania a chance. I couldn't be worse off than I was now, so I would have nothing to lose by going with him.

A couple he knew drove us to Brooklyn, to 416 Clinton Avenue, which was headquarters for Teen Challenge. There I was both greeted and screened by Dave Wilkerson's brother, Don, by two other ministers and by Ruth Cowgill, the dean of women.

As the screening progressed, I became, first, alarmed for fear I'd be rejected because of my past. Then I got mad, especially when Don Wilkerson began asking me how I'd supported my addiction.

"That's none of your business, man," I snapped, glaring at him stonily.

"Young lady," he answered, "if that's your attitude, we don't want you here."

Okay; so once again I wasn't wanted. I'd been rejected more than once before, so I wasn't surprised that Don would reject me too, and, as was always the case when I felt rejected, I turned hostile.

"Okay," I yelled, "Keep your damned Teen Challenge. You don't want me and I don't want you." And, on that note, I headed for the door.

But, before I could walk away from what might be

my final opportunity for survival, good sense took over.

Here I was, a messed up junkie with no help in sight, unless it was the help I might get here. And in some way I realized that these people, like Nicky Cruz, really wanted to help me. I couldn't understand why, but they did.

So reluctantly I went back to Don and apologized. "Let me stay," I begged, "because I do want to break my habit. You said that Jesus can help me, and I need and want that help."

The staff members looked at me and at one another undecidedly. Even though their faith in the Lord was strong, they must have been wondering whether it was equal to the challenge I presented. To begin with, they didn't even have a place for me to sleep until Ruth, bless her, volunteered, "Don, she can have my bed."

At that, it was settled that I would remain at Teen Challenge in the care of new friends who'd pray for me and help me through the ordeal of withdrawal from cold turkey for what we all hoped would be the last time.

As I fell asleep on Ruth's bed, I was too high and too exhausted to think much about the next day or the next week or anything else. But when I awoke the next morning, knowing that I was going to have to kick one more time without any medication, I briefly wondered whether I wouldn't be better off at Rockland. The past few times I'd kicked cold turkey, I'd gone into convulsions which put me into the hospital, and I didn't want to go through that again.

Mustering my wits, I told myself that the only sensible thing to do would be to get into my dirty jeans and shirt and hit the street in search of drugs before the withdrawal symptoms began. Groggily, I looked for my clothes. But they were nowhere to be found. Nor was my knife.

Gone. My knife was gone. And I certainly didn't want to hit the streets without it.

Fuzzily, I recalled that the night before Ruth had hugged me, making me intensely nervous with her outbursts of "Praise Jesus" and "Jesus loves you, Cookie." While she was embracing me, she must have lifted my knife. Pretty tricky, I thought, as I burst out with a string of oaths.

Well, I thought, no matter where they'd hidden my clothes, I was going to find them—and my knife of course—and split out of there.

But just then I realized something was in the room that hadn't been there the night before. It was a new dress. Fresh and pretty, it looked as though it might be too big for my skinny, eighty-five pound body, but it was so inviting that I had to try it on. I hadn't had a new dress in so long that I wasn't sure when I'd worn one last.

Examining myself in the mirror I was pleased by what I saw. In the inexpensive but pretty dress I didn't look like Crazy Cookie, the strung-out junkie who was so mad that other junkies were afraid of her. I actually looked like a terribly thin but not unattractive girl dressed for school or a job, or even church.

Inexplicably, I felt no incipient withdrawal pains. In fact, I felt pretty good, so I went down to breakfast.

While I was wolfing down my food, the people around me were praising Jesus and thanking Him for what He'd done for me. They really did seem crazy, I thought, but there was no question about it—They knew some wonderful secret which had gotten me through withdrawal with no discomfort.

Were they spiritualists maybe, I wondered. Whatever their power might be, I was going to stick around and find out more about it. Because it was pretty wonderful, I had decided.

It took me quite a while, however, to learn just how wonderful that power could be.

CHAPTER 16

Tears of Joy

I'd been in jail, and other institutions, so many times that I fit right into the regulated life of Teen Challenge.

Almost.

At other times and in other places, I'd had to discipline myself to conform to rules—rules laid down by madhouse matrons, rules laid down by prison guards. I'd conformed in order to survive.

So when I discovered that Teen Challenge had rules too, and that one of the rules was that you either shape up or ship out, I disciplined myself to obey, for I really wanted to stick around at least long enough to discover the source of the staff's magical power. Their prayers had taken me off drugs without withdrawal symptoms. So they obviously knew something I ought to find out about.

And besides, if I left Teen Challenge, I'd have to sleep on the sidewalks again instead of in a comfortable bed. Thus, every instinct told me to abide by the regulations and stay put.

Still there was one rule I simply couldn't obey— the rule against smoking. No matter how hard I tried (and I didn't try very hard), I absolutely couldn't give up cigarettes.

Despite this shortcoming, the Teen Challenge counselors continued to treat me with loving kindness as they talked to me about Jesus, the Son of God who'd died for my sins, because He loved me so much.

Jesus. . .

When I tried to concentrate on who and what He might be, I could only think of the baby in nativity scenes at Christmas, the one we'd sung about once a year when I was a child in Puerto Rico.

Although I was told every day that the Son of God could make my scarlet sins as white as snow and that He loved me no matter what I'd done, I simply couldn't believe it.

My past was simply too horrendous to be forgiven. And, through it, I'd become too de-humanized to react to the concept of love. Because I couldn't feel anything for anybody, I couldn't imagine how the Lord Himself could feel anything for me—anything except perhaps white hot anger because of my wickedness.

My ideas of religion were still entangled with the spiritualist indoctrination I'd received as a child. Therefore, I thought that there probably was a giant Something, somewhere, ready to wreak terrible vengeance whenever I displeased it.

But as for a God of love—I understood nothing about either God or perfect love.

Nina, I remembered, had loved me. She'd loved me so much, in fact, that she'd forgiven me a great deal. But finally even she had become so disgusted by my deception and depravity that she'd washed her hands of me. Nina—even doting Nina—thought I was a hopeless case.

So how could this Jesus, whom the staff kept talking about, forgive me of all my sins and love me in spite of them? The premise just didn't make sense. Further, suppose this Jesus really did love me with such a cleansing love, could I love Him in return?

All Nina had gotten in exchange for her forgiving devotion was either indifference or contempt, a chilly distaste for the stupidity which allowed her to forgive such a hard case as myself.

At the staff's urging, I'd sometimes say, "Jesus, come into my heart," but so far as I could tell, nothing happened.

Nothing at all.

I'd sit as part of a group and hear others who'd come to Teen Challenge telling how Christ had changed their lives, how He'd set them free from wicked pasts, how He'd rescued them from drug habits and how sorry they were for all their sins. Sometimes during these confessions, the repentant sinner would weep. Then I'd feel emotion, embarrassment. For I'd never experienced true remorse for anything I'd done.

In prostitute court, I'd felt shame, yes, but never a weight of guilt. I'd done what circumstances had forced me to do. I hadn't liked doing it but it had been necessary, so I didn't feel remorseful.

Weeping sinners at Teen Challenge were a novelty which made me uncomfortable. I, who couldn't cry over anything, was appalled by the spectacle of young men sobbing because they'd offended their Savior.

Though the Teen Challenge program wasn't getting through to me, it didn't occur to me that this was my own fault.

Jesus isn't changing me, I thought, either because I'm such a mess that even He can't renew me, or because He just doesn't want to be bothered. Plenty of people, my own relatives included, had written me off as more trouble than I was worth, so I couldn't blame this Jesus if He felt the same way.

Teen Challenge had given me wholesome food, a clean place to sleep, a painless withdrawal from drugs, and a new dress. That was it. But I'd gotten more than I could rightfully expect. Therefore, I decided, as soon as I gained a little more weight, I'd cut out.

Meanwhile, turned hostile by my conclusion that Jesus, too, had rejected me, I became my old, unruly self—encouraging fights among the girls in the program. Once, after I'd tried to throw a girl down the stairs, I was sure I'd be asked to leave.

But, exercising incredible patience, the staff lectured me and allowed me to stay.

In the meantime, changing seasons encouraged me to delay my split from Teen Challenge, for winter was coming and I didn't like the idea of working the cold streets of New York. So I continued to accept the hospitality of my patient new friends, while I made their lives increasingly difficult.

Finally, I was told that I would be moved to a residence for girls at Rhinebeck, New York, to which girls were "promoted" after they'd been in the Teen Challenge program for awhile.

At first, the idea of moving to a new place was appealing because I'd never seen any of the United States outside New York City and Rockland. And I was curious as to what sort of a place Rhinebeck might be.

So it was with a spirit of adventure that I set out for my new home. When I saw it, however, I was horrified.

The girls' residence was a desolate old mansion on the Hudson River and, to my ghetto-oriented mind, it seemed as remote from the rest of Society as the

South Pole. How in the world would I pass the time in a place like this, I couldn't help but wonder. Well, I concluded, I wouldn't. I'd been planning to cut out of Teen Challenge anyway, and this move to Rhinebeck would trigger the action. Rather than stay in such a barren, unpromising locale, I'd run away and go back to the life I'd known on the streets of the city.

That was my decision. Yet, before I could put this plan into action, news of another potential adventure stayed me.

We would be going to Pittsburgh, I was informed.

Pittsburgh! If I'd been told I was going to Paris, I could hardly have been more intrigued, for Pittsburgh was not only a different city from New York, it was in a different state! I'd never crossed a state line, and I didn't want to miss this opportunity.

Thus I decided to stay with Teen Challenge, at least until I'd seen Pittsburgh and Pennsylvania.

The famous evangelist and healer Kathryn Kuhlman was the reason for the trip. She and Dave Wilkerson were friends and, as a result of that friendship, he'd held a meeting at the Syria Mosque in Pittsburgh where Miss Kuhlman also held her services.

Now Miss Kuhlman and Dave were organizing a giant youth rally there which all the girls from the Rhinebeck residence plus all the boys from the Teen Challenge farm in Rehrersberg, Pennsylvania, were to attend, traveling to the site by bus. While I didn't care much about the youth rally, I did look forward to the prospect of being in a crowd of young people. The day might provide a real kick, I decided.

Yet I never dreamt what a kick it would actually be! The big auditorium was packed with kids of all colors, sizes and descriptions. . .all so alive with expectation that their excitement began to affect me.

Kathryn Kuhlman's choir sang beautifully, and then several people told about their encounters with Jesus Who'd relieved them of all their burdens and made them new and whole.

All that sounded great and would have stirred a response in me if I hadn't been convinced that not even Jesus cared for a prostitute junkie. Still, as Dave began to preach, I found myself listening hungrily, expectantly.

I'd never heard him speak to a crowd before, and the power of his voice was surprising to me. But his message surprised me even more because he seemed to be speaking directly to me. It was as though we were in a one-to-one conversation, and he was giving me instructions and advice I badly needed. He was saying that a lot of people are phonies, and I was nodding in agreement, because I'd known plenty in my time. But then he seemed to be reminding me that I, too, was a phony.

And, surprisingly, I found myself agreeing with that also. I'd hung around Teen Challenge under false pretenses. I'd pretended to invite Jesus into my heart when, in all honesty, I hadn't expected Him to come and wasn't sure that I even wanted Him. Dave was talking about being a phony before God, and that was exactly what I'd been.

If I'd drop my smart-aleck cynicism, I'd have to admit that I, too, wanted a Savior. I wanted a cleansing. I wanted to be healed of all past hurts. I wanted a new life—complete with a new heart which could feel for other people. Like those repentant sinners whose tears had embarrassed me so, I wanted to be able to cry.

As the choir began the invitational hymn, I bowed my head and, for the first time in my life, I talked to the Lord sincerely and directly—though I must admit, rather awkwardly. "Jesus," I said politely, "if you are real, I want you to do me a favor. Please.

"I want to be part of the human race again, a person who can laugh and love other people, and shed tears. Jesus, please, if you love me. . .please, Lord, make me cry."

When the Lord answered, I didn't hear a clap of thunder or see fire in a burning bush, but I heard Him speak as clearly as Moses heard God's voice on the desert and on the mountain. He was telling me that I was, indeed, a miserable sinner. One by one, all my misdeeds were recounted, my neglect of Dondi, my disregard for Nina, my lies and my abuse of self.

Yet, at the same time, he told me that He loved me even more than the people at Teen Challenge had said He did. His love was too large for words to describe but, as I communed with Jesus, it warmed and comforted me.

As I remembered my sins, I was, for the first time ever, filled with such a feeling of guilt that my eyes brimmed with tears. Sorry—oh how sorry I was for all the terrible things that I'd done!

Tears, I knew, couldn't wash those sins away, but the blood of Jesus could. "I am real," Jesus assured me, "and I'll make a new creature of you."

At this reassurance, I shook with sobs. I was weeping with remorse, because of my past, but I was also crying with joy because, at long last, I had a future!

CHAPTER 17

The Devil Won't Quit

Just as Christ had reached out to prove He was real through my tears, the devil promptly reached out to prove that he, too, was real through my doubts.

The trip back from Pennsylvania began noisily as young bus passengers sang and shouted out the happiness they'd found through knowing the Lord. My counselors, joyously praising the Lord, were particularly jubilant, for they'd seen me cry and welcomed my tears of penance as first evidence of a changed life.

But I wasn't shouting and singing. I was excited because of what I'd undergone, yet at the same time I was pensive and confused, for the devil was prodding me to ask myself: "How do you know you met Jesus? Is it really possible to meet someone you can't physically touch and see?

"Your father was mentally unbalanced, or he wouldn't have killed himself, and maybe you're crazy too. Are you sure the encounter with Jesus was real, or were you imagining something the way you used to imagine things on the streets of New York City?"

The closer the bus drew to Rhinebeck, the hazier my recollection of repentance became. Something very pleasant had happened to me, true. But within only a few hours, the episode was dimming. . . becoming more like a dream than a reality. And, within a few days, it had become almost like something that happened to another person.

I'd been promised that, after inviting Jesus into my heart, I'd be a new creature. Yet it seemed to me that I was still the same flawed Cookie—angry, dispirited, causing trouble for those around me. I even continued smoking on the sly, though Teen Challenge strictly forbade the use of cigarettes. If I'd actually met Jesus, why wasn't He changing me, I wondered. Why, oh, why couldn't I retain the rapturous sense of being loved that I'd known in Pittsburgh?

Despite my doubts, however, I continued to believe that I had encountered the Lord, and I began to search the Bible for scripture to confirm my conviction. I wanted to know more about Jesus. I wanted to be told again and again, until I was thoroughly convinced that He truly did love me and had forgiven every one of my sins.

But my attempts to read the Bible didn't tell me a thing because my misused brain, so long befuddled with drugs, couldn't make heads or tails out of the great Good News. It even rejected the simple, reassuring promise found in John 3:16, "For God so loved the world. . ." I read it but I couldn't remember it, even after I'd determined to memorize the glorious pledge.

". . . that whosoever believeth in Him should not perish but have everlasting life." The words were beautiful but beyond my grasp until, after three weeks of determined concentration, I was able to memorize them, to repeat them for own encouragement and comfort.

Still I was unable to regain the wonderful feeling I'd known in Pittsburgh. Intellectually, I could convince myself that Jesus was real, but emotionally I was a blank. Where was the holy joy which made other people shout and sing?

I tried talking with the Lord as I'd done at the Kathryn Kuhlman meeting but, even as I prayed, my mind wandered. The words I spoke seemed to hit the ceiling and bounce back down before they ever reached God!

Remaining rebellious, I was lazy and unfulfilled. Only one thing in my life had changed since my Pittsburgh experience. Now, at long last, I did have a conscience.

I sincerely wanted to please Christ and, when I realized I was failing Him, I was sorry. Nevertheless, I continued to fail.

One of my outstanding failures was in the field of assigned housework which I found boring and hateful.

As a part of our rehabilitation, each girl at Teen Challenge was expected to conform to a schedule and perform certain tasks. Every morning after breakfast, we went to Chapel, and afterward into a period of Bible study. After lunch we did various chores, or rather we were expected to do them. A period of prayer and meditation interrupted this work detail, after which we allegedly got back to our labors.

"Allegedly" was a word particularly appropriate for my efforts, for I was so bored by the light housework I was asked to do that I tackled it in an indifferent fashion. When I dusted, I simply flicked my cloth at the dust, most of which remained as it was, whereupon my counselor, Sharon Webb, would make me dust over again.

Because Sharon was everything I wasn't, I couldn't stand her and I did my best to provoke her.

A cool, tall, lovely blonde, she was a registered nurse who'd volunteered to work one summer at Teen Challenge, and had remained to become a counselor. Her appearance and manner were practically letterperfect, and so was the standard of conduct she set for me. If a rule existed, I was to obey it, for the discipline imposed by Teen Challenge was part of its carefully-thought-out and tested rehabilitation program.

Therefore, if dust lay in the area assigned to my keeping, I was to remove it, for cleanliness—whether it was next to Godliness or not—was at least a very good thing.

That was Sharon's attitude, and it aggravated me no end. Sloppy and insecure, I resented her self-control and the inner peace she found through Christ.

The very fact Sharon wanted me to do something was enough to turn me against doing it. Instead of accepting her guidance without question, I sullenly rejected it.

Meanwhile, I'd given up trying to break my cigarette habit, though I pretended I had. I never smoked when I might be seen, but each night, in the secrecy of my dark room, I sat by the window contentedly inhaling the tobacco smoke and exhaling out the window. After all, had Jesus said a word against smoking? Not on your life! I'd searched the Scriptures without finding a single occasion on which He'd condemned cigarettes.

That was my reasoning, completely by-passing the real issue which was one of self-discipline and honesty.

I would have liked to have given up cigarettes if I could have done so without great effort. But I was still putting my own selfish pleasure above the debt I owed to the Teen Challenge program. Often, as I puffed, I suffered from a guilty conscience, because, whether the Bible said anything about cigarettes or not, I knew that I was living a lie when I tried to deceive the Teen Challenge staff.

So, during those moments when I was burdened with guilt, I'd turn accusingly toward Jesus. "Why don't you help me?" I'd fume. "You've made me want to do what's right but You don't supply me the strength to do it.

"You haven't changed my life at all. You've only made me feel worse, because now I'm sorry when I do the wrong thing. And I don't think that's fair.

"Jesus, are you there? Are you listening? If You are, why do I feel so miserable?"

For I was indeed miserable much of the time. Having learned to cry, I was often on the verge of tears, ready to weep over my own shortcomings, ready to weep because past mistakes had separated me from Nina, and especially ready to weep because at long last I was consumed with a mother's yearning for her child.

Curiously, though I'd never really known Dondi, I missed him. Legally, I had no right to him. Still I wanted him with me.

CHAPTER 18

Jesus' Strange Instruction

"Cookie!" Groggily, I rubbed my sleep-ladened eyes as I tried to determine who it was calling me, and why.

Was it morning already? No, my room was still pitch black, but someone was calling me. Was I supposed to get up now, in the middle of the night?

"Cookie," the voice called again, "I need you. I want you to work for me." And then I knew who was speaking, as clearly as old Eli had identified the voice which called to young Samuel.

Christ was calling me, letting me know that He was not only real but that He had a personal concern and use for me. Me. . .of all people!

"Yes, Jesus," I cried. "I'm so glad You're speaking to me again. What do You want me to do?"

"I want you to work with young people," He told me.

Well, that surprised me even more than the voice itself had done, because I seemed less prepared than anyone in the world to help my peers. Why, I couldn't even handle my own life, my temper, my rebelliousness, my sloth. Yet I had heard Jesus' voice clearly telling me, "I want you to work with young people," and it had scarcely faded before the pains of all the young people I'd known began to burden me.

I thought of all the girls on the streets, of the young men who were destroying their minds and bodies through drug use, of the hostile, hardened gang members who placed no value upon human life, including their own. And I began to sob.

"Oh, Jesus," I wept, "I do want to work for You and I do want to help young people, but I don't know how. Please show me how to help You and them. And please come to me again."

After that I went back to sleep, but the next morning when I awoke the midnight experience was still vivid. How, I kept wondering, was I supposed to help young people?

The whole idea of Cookie—undisciplined Cookie who still sneaked cigarettes—leading others to the Lord was so outrageous that I didn't dare tell anyone about the voice I'd heard. Further, my attitude toward Teen Challenge and Sharon remained so negative that no one on the staff could have suspected that Jesus had called me to do special work for Him.

As a matter of fact, I taunted Sharon one day until I seriously jeopardized my chances to stay in the Teen Challenge program. As usual, she was accusing me of smoking and then of lying to her about it. And, as usual, I'd flared back at her with suggestions that she wasn't much of a Christian or she wouldn't be so suspicious of me.

Finally, her patience almost exhausted, Sharon told me, "Cookie, don't you know that we've considered asking you to leave? Your lies and disobedience could cost you your place in the program. So please try hard to change."

I was scared, yet furious.

"So throw me out," I challenged. "Just throw me out. I don't like living here anyway."

Fortunately for me, while I was fuming and storming over my differences with Sharon, she was praying over them. While I was clutching my resentment tightly, mentally gnawing on it like a dog gnawing over a spent bone, she was holding our breach up to God, begging Him to heal it.

And, since the Lord loves us and answers the prayers of the faithful, He began to cure the rift between my counselor and me. Sharon's attitude toward me, as well as my attitude toward her, began to improve so that, while we didn't become instantly close, we did begin to talk with each other without fireworks. She'd stop by my room sometimes and ask me questions about Dondi, not in an offensive, meddlesome manner but in a manner of concern which convinced me she was sincerely interested in my little boy. And she told me more about herself and her own struggle to grow as a Christian.

She prayed for me and with me until, quite gradually, I accepted her as a sister in Christ.

One day as we talked, Sharon amazed me by saying, "Cookie, I've been talking with the Lord quite a lot about what you should do with your future and He's told me that He has a special job for you to do. I don't know what the work will be, but I am sure that God is going to assign you to a special and important task."

Well, if I'd needed anything to reassure me that Jesus had spoken to me one night and told me that He wanted me to work with young people, Sharon's revelation was it. Even then, I didn't tell her that Jesus had spoken to me too about my future, but I happily joined her in praying for a further revelation.

Meanwhile, my longing to see Dondi was increasing daily, as was the desire to see my grand-mother again.

I'd written Nina about my conversion in Pitts-burgh and asked her to forgive me for all the ways I'd wronged and hurt her. But for weeks she hadn't answered a word, which wasn't too surprising, in view of the fact she could neither read nor write.

I finally received a letter written for her by someone else in which she told me she was glad I was happy and out of New York. "Stay out of New York," Nina advised.

This wasn't a very encouraging first step toward reconciliation. Still I was pleased to have heard from Nina at all. On the other hand, my unsatisfactory family relationship continued to depress me.

I wanted to set things completely right with Nina. I wanted to see my baby, to make up to him for the way I'd neglected him, to give him a chance to know me now that I was off drugs and in touch with the Lord. Sharon sensed all this and, in addition to praying about it, took a practical step to bring results.

One day I was called into the office of Brother Mitchell, director of the girls' residence, and given an amazing piece of news.

"Cookie," he said, "Sharon has told us how concerned you are about your son and how much you'd like to see him. We've been discussing this, and we think you might grow faster as a Christian if he were here with you for awhile. Would you like for him to come here?"

Would I like it? I was ecstatic at the mere thought that Dondi might spend a day with me.

But Brother Mitchell was planning something more. Somehow he made contact with Nina and convinced her that it would be perfectly all right for

Dondi to pay a long visit to his errant mother in Rhinebeck.

So at last I had my baby with me, and a prouder mother you've never seen! He was so beautiful. . .so chubby. . .so sweet. Everytime I looked at him I was stunned by the realization that a half-crazy, teenaged junkie had borne such a perfectly adorable little boy. It was astonishing!

And equally astonishing was Dondi's attitude toward me, for, even though he'd seldom seen me in all his four years, and then under the most unattractive conditions, he accepted me immediately as his mother. He gave me his love, though I'd done nothing to earn it.

Nina, of course, had to be reassured that Dondi was safe with me and my new associates so, shortly after he arrived at Rhinebeck, she arrived too. though only for a brief visit.

She still wore her hair—now white—in a severe bun. She still looked at me through dark, searching eyes in which I saw a suspicion that my cure wouldn't be permanent. But she didn't berate me for past mistakes, and she didn't take my Dondi away.

"Stay out of New York," she ordered, never adding that she loved me in spite of everything. Somehow I felt that perhaps she did and, in time, we'd become close again.

My life, which had been such a mess, was straightening out so beautifully and I credited God for the miracles which brought this about. Still I wasn't as happy as I should have been.

I hadn't mustered the strength to conquer the habit of smoking, so I still had to lie about my cigarette habit. I tried praying regularly but, almost as regularly, I experienced the discouraging feeling that God wasn't there.

My Bible continued to be a mystery to me, in large part, and I never had the uncontrollable desire to shout "Hallelujah" or "Thank you, Jesus" the way some people did. If the people around me weren't exhibiting overt joy because of their relationship with the Lord, they were at least evidencing a deep contentment.

Yet I felt neither. Something was missing in my spiritual life and I had no idea how to go about finding it.

I knew that Sharon and Dave and most of the staff at Teen Challenge were Pentecostals which, in my Roman Catholic-oriented opinion, made them a little bit weird. When they worshipped, they were inclined to sing and cry out, holding up their hands in a way that turned me off. They also talked a lot about the baptism of the Holy Spirit which they highly recommended and which, I assumed, made them behave as they did.

But not wanting to act this way, I neglected to ask the Lord to give me this baptism.

Then one morning in Chapel, Brother Mitchell said something which got my utmost attention and stirred a desire for this strange blessing that my friends had received. He talked of a time in his life when, although he'd loved the Lord, he hadn't been able to live the way that he should or that he wanted to live. He hadn't possessed the power to fight off the devil, he said, until he'd asked God to grant him the baptism of the Holy Spirit.

But when he'd received the baptism, he'd received such a generous measure of Christ's love that he'd found new strength to resist temptations.

Well, I concluded, if that was what the baptism did for a person, then I sure did need it. However, another part of Brother Mitchell's message had left me wary.

Along with the baptism, he said, he'd received a new prayer language, one which I wasn't convinced I'd really want. I'd heard my Pentecostal friends speaking in what they called "tongues," which sounded to me like some sort of gibberish they were "inventing."

In any case, I didn't want to prattle like an idiot, and I decided, if baptism of the Holy Spirit meant I'd have to pray in tongues, I'd just as soon leave the whole thing alone.

Nevertheless, Brother Mitchell's talk had moved me and stirred my curiosity. Would this baptism make me as happy as Sharon and Dave. . .as strong as they were in the face of temptation? The question recurringly crossed my mind. Especially when I was threatened with expulsion from the program which had taken me off drugs and given me back my baby.

One night as I sat by my window sneaking a forbidden cigarette and watching Dondi sleep, I faced the depressing prospect that my little boy and I might lose our haven and be sent back to Nina in New York, simply because I couldn't break my tobacco habit.

"Oh, Jesus," I pleaded, "won't you help me, please? You've done so much for me already, but I need more. Please send me strength. Please save me from myself. Oh, Jesus, what I need is another miracle. Please, please give me just one more."

And the Savior, who'd already done such wonderful things for me, heard and answered through the Third Person of the Trinity, the Holy Spirit.

Morning would find me a totally changed person, finally sampling the fullness of God's grace.

CHAPTER 19

The Holy Spirit

As I sat by the window, smoking and praying, the incongruity of what I was doing almost made me laugh.

Or cry.

How dare I tell Jesus that I loved Him and call on Him for a miracle while half of my mind was worrying about an impending cigarette shortage? My tobacco supply was almost exhausted. In fact, I was smoking my very last cigarette so, even as I prayed, I was wondering where and how soon I could get a fresh supply.

"Cookie," I chided myself, "you're one horrible mess. You're disgusting. You're going to get Dondi and yourself kicked out of here. . .then what will become of you?

Frightened and disgusted, I confronted the question to which I had no comforting answer.

I was drawing deeply on the last half of my last cigarette, hungrily savoring each lungful of flavor. But I didn't finish the smoke. Instead, on sudden impulse, I tossed the cigarette fragment out the window, and once again tried to pray.

"Jesus," I called. . ."Jesus."

Beyond saying His name, I was speechless.

Sharon had told me about a man who'd been moved to accept Christ through repeating Jesus' name over and over, and the recollection of this story encouraged me to keep repeating it too.

"Jesus. Jesus. Jesus." I couldn't say anything else but, gradually, as I addressed the Savior, a feeling of calm swept over me. I was happy, because I was sure that Jesus was listening. He wasn't visible; He didn't speak to me as He'd done in the past, but He was a presence, soothing and encouraging me with His love.

"Jesus. Jesus. Jesus."

I don't know how many times I said the name before I found myself saying more. ..

"Jesus, I love you. I really do. Gloria a Cristo. Hallelujah. Bendito sea Tu Nombre. I love you, Jesus." In both English and Spanish I kept praising the Lord, thanking Him for His gifts, above all for my salvation. Minutes were flying by and then hours as I prayed. . .in English and in Spanish. . .in Spanish and in English.

And, finally, in another language I'd never heard before and couldn't understand. The words meant nothing to me and yet, as I spoke them, I knew that I was presenting a perfect petition to God. Something was putting those words in my mouth, leading me to pour out my longing and joy in a torrent of phrases I couldn't decipher but which, I was certain, were being understood and welcomed in heaven.

Was this the work of the Holy Spirit, I wondered.

When I'd heard my Pentecostal friends speaking in strange tongues, I'd thought they sounded ridiculous, if not downright mad, but now, as I spoke in a strange tongue, I felt neither foolish nor crazy.

Basically, I felt great. Absolutely great. In fact, I'd never felt better in my whole life.

I got very little sleep that night, for I prayed until almost dawn. Yet I was up early, laughing and lively, which in itself was proof that a miracle had occurred. For in the past I'd arisen sullenly and only when someone had prodded me out of bed.

I was indeed a new creature, the kind the Scripture had promised I could be through Christ. The change in me was so apparent that, when I reported for breakfast, Mrs. Mitchell exclaimed, "Well, just look at Cookie. Look at her smile. Something wonderful must have happened to her."

Stammeringly, I admitted that it had. "I think," I confessed, "that I've received the baptism of the Holy Spirit."

Mrs. Mitchell accepted this information without reservation, for I was so obviously changed that she, too, was sure the Holy Spirit had brought about the transformation.

At chapel that morning, I couldn't wait to jump up and share my experience with all my friends so, when the time came for personal testimony, I was the first to volunteer.

However, when I got to my feet, I was speechless again. I said, "Praise the Lord," but beyond that I couldn't say a thing in either Spanish or English. Then, though, without conscious effort on my part, the new, strange language began to pour out of my mouth, just as it had done the night before. And, as had been the case earlier, I knew that I was saying something acceptable to Jesus.

As I spoke, others in the chapel audience began to shout and cry, joining me in praising our Heavenly Father. And, when I was at last silent, they enfolded me with their Christian love.

After I was baptized by the Spirit, I was no longer haunted by the fear that my confrontations with Jesus had been imaginary or isolated experiences I might not enjoy again. At last I knew that He would be with me always, and this knowledge gave me the power to live a happier and more productive life.

I no longer despised my tasks but went about them singing. Prayer and Bible Study no longer seemed too long but rather too short. And the Bible passages which I hadn't understood before were now clear, thanks to the insight the Spirit had given me.

As a result, I couldn't get enough of Bible reading.

Meanwhile, I completely lost interest in smoking. So the half cigarette I'd tossed away turned out to be my last. Thinking about that, I decided it had turned out to be the trigger which activated my spiritual baptism. For I hadn't asked the Holy Spirit to deluge me with this extra blessing. Actually, I'd looked rather askance upon those who'd received it.

But, when I'd chosen God's will over that final half-a-smoke, the Holy Spirit had rewarded me with a bounty of gifts.

Soon after receiving my spiritual baptism without asking for it, I received something else which I had asked for:

An opportunity to help young people as Christ had instructed me to do. For one morning, to my utter amazement and disbelief, Dave Wilkerson told me that he wanted me to be a junior counselor for Teen Challenge during the coming summer.

Me? I, who'd only known Christ for a few months after so many years of devil-hatched depravity, seemed such an unlikely fisherman to go seining for straying souls! Yet Dave told me that was what he wanted me to do, to go fishing for the lost in my old neighborhood in the Bronx.

"We are about to start our summer evangelism program," he said, "and we want you to speak at some street rallies in the Bronx. Do you think you are ready to share with others the things God has done for you?"

Without the slightest comprehension of what all the repercussions might be, I gave a prompt "yes." Thrilled and flattered to have been offered such responsibility, I was so ignorant of what I might be letting myself in for that I had instantly agreed to hit the streets as the newest representative of Teen Challenge.

"Fine," Dave said, smiling at me. "Someone will bring you back into our headquarters on Clinton Street next week and we'll get the summer program underway."

I'd only been in the rehabilitation program for three months, whereas Sharon and the other counselors had been solid Christians all of their lives. But, as I walked back to my room, I didn't feel at all hesitant about going into the slums as a missionary to youth.

When I got to my room, though, I was brought up short by a sudden thought:

Dondi.

If I went back to Clinton Avenue, what would become of him?

He was sitting on the floor, playing happily, a perfect picture of healthy, good-humored innocence. How in the world could I bear to send him back to Nina? For that's what I'd have to do if I moved back into the city to speak at Bronx rallies. Since I'd been declared an unfit mother, Nina, who was his legal guardian, had been reluctant to let me keep him at all. When she found out I was going to move him from rural Rhinebeck back into New York, she'd insist that I return him to her. And I'd probably have to do that anyway, because there wouldn't be room for him at the Teen Challenge headquarters, nor would there be anyone to take care of him there while I was working at street meetings.

"Oh, my darling baby," I wept inwardly, "how can I let you go? Now that you've accepted me as your mother, what will you think of me if I seem to abandon you again? And since you're thriving so in the country, how can I send you back to the ghetto?"

For a wild instant I entertained the idea of grabbing Dondi and running away from Teen Challenge, from Nina, from the prospect of separation from my son.

Instead, as I communed with Him through prayer, He reminded me, "Cookie, I took care of Dondi all the years you were on drugs. When you didn't care about him, I did. And I still do. So while you're doing my work, trust Me to protect your child.

"Don't worry about Dondi. Worry, instead, about all the young people in the streets who've never met Me."

I listened to the Lord and believed His promise. So the next week found Dondi back at Nina's and me heading out from Clinton Avenue into the heart of the Bronx which I'd left less than half a year before as an eighty-five pound, mentally ill, physically filthy junkie.

Now I was up to 125 pounds. My complexion and eyes were clear and my hair was clean. I was wearing a bright summer dress, totally different from the soiled rags I'd worn on the streets. But, best of all, I was wearing the armor of God, for I was going out as one of His warriors, confident that He'd protect me from the devil.

The devil, however, was setting up some cleverly laid ambushes. And one was to prove almost fatal.

CHAPTER 20

Close Call or Flight From Salvation

Plunging into my Teen Challenge work, I soon discovered that my old friends weren't so much a danger to me as my new ones. They didn't mean to harm or threaten me, of course, for they sincerely cared about me and wanted only the best for me. Nevertheless, it was my fellow workers from Teen Challenge who came closest to destroying me.

The first night I went back into the Bronx to testify about the changes Jesus had made in my life, I was welcomed by Sam, a burly black who'd been a part of the very worst portion of my life. "Hey, Cookie," he shouted, thrusting two huge arms around me and literally lifting me off my feet. "Where have you been? I thought maybe you were dead, after all.

"And how come you're so fat?"

He grinned slyly as he wagged me back and forth like a rag doll. "Oh, no," I thought, "The kids from Teen Challenge who are watching this must really be shocked."

For my companions in the summer ministry were, for the most part, clean-cut boys and girls from Middle America who, through their love for the

Lord, had volunteered to spend a summer working for Jesus.

As Sam hugged me, I caught a glimpse of young eyes wide with amazement, of rosy, young faces blank with surprise.

"Put her down," Dave Wilkerson ordered Sam. "She's not the Cookie you used to know. She now belongs to God."

Sam was so stunned by this pronouncement that he did put me down as he stared at me, trying to figure out just what Dave meant.

"What's that crazy white man talking about?" he inquired of me.

"He's telling you that a miracle has happened," I answered. "I do belong to Jesus now, and He's made a new person of me."

Sam couldn't have looked more disgusted if I'd said I became a stoolie for the cops. Shaking his head, he turned and disappeared into an alley.

Meanwhile Dave was organizing the meeting which was attracting a tatty and generally disinterested crowd who came into the streets mostly to get out of their hot tenement rooms.

They'd gathered in the same way to see me knife Officer Harris. In that neighborhood, residents would gather just as eagerly to see a killing as to hear the Gospel preached.

The hope of salvation wasn't the magnet drawing our audience which was composed mainly of junkies, prostitutes, petty thieves and other assorted derelicts.

Our young volunteers got the program underway with a series of gospel songs. I knew what the neighborhood must be thinking of them and their music because I knew what I would have thought of such a covey of clean-cut hymn singers only a few months earlier.

Suddenly their singing was almost interrupted—almost but not quite—by a barrage of water-filled balloons plummeting from a nearby rooftop. Looking up, I could see a group of Black Muslims lobbing the missiles.

"Nobody will ever listen to us with this going on," I thought. "We don't have a chance to be heard."

However, I was reckoning with the power of God, for despite the balloons and other disturbances, the crowd was beginning to settle down.

Dave was speaking now about the woman caught in adultery who'd been forgiven by Jesus, and his message was getting through to his audience.

Then it was my turn to speak. I quickly strengthened myself with a silent prayer before turning my attention to the guys with the balloons.

"Hey, you up on the roof," I yelled. "Come on down and let me tell you something. You know me. Cookie Rodriguez. Most of you know me." And I began to address various people by name as I spotted familiar faces among the crowd.

"You know what I was, don't you? I was probably even worse than the worst of you. Some of you were afraid of me, weren't you?

"Okay, then. Let me tell you how I've changed and who made the change possible."

And with that, I began to talk about Jesus and the wonderful ways in which He'd blessed me.

As I talked, I began to cry, though I tried very hard not to, for in that neighborhood tears were scorned as a sign of weakness. Nevertheless, my eyes were overflowing as I continued with my story.

The response from the crowd was overwhelming. Nudged by the Holy Spirit, even the Black Muslims came down and joined in prayer.

During the summer, I had the privilege of seeing many people respond to Jesus at Teen Challenge meetings. Yet I never saw such a great response as that at my first rally.

Other meetings were almost as successful, however, and this should have made me perfectly happy, but I wasn't because of the attitude of some of my fellow workers.

At the Clinton Avenue Teen Challenge Headquarters, I'd found two new solidly comforting friends to replace Sharon whom I'd left behind at Rhinebeck. One was Ruth Cowgill who'd welcomed me so warmly the night One-Eye Dutch had brought me in from the street.

The other was Ingrid Thatcher, a lovely blonde of Norwegian descent whose parents lived in South Dakota and who was on hiatus from a teaching assignment in Colorado.

Ingrid, like Sharon, grew up in a Christian home, so she'd known Jesus all her life and was well equipped and willing to help me grow in the Lord. Her faith included a belief that I sincerely loved Christ and had been permanently freed from my drug addiction.

However, not all my colleagues were equally convinced that my redemption was viable.

At first I, too, was a little nervous lest I backslide when I was faced with the temptations of my old neighborhood. But after I took a group from Teen Challenge to a "shooting gallery," a basement in which junkies congregated to shoot heroin, I knew that I was clean for keeps.

The basement room was littered and foul-smelling with human filth. Vomit stains streaked the walls against which junkies lolled, not even conscious that we were looking at them. Rats scurried back and forth across recumbent forms of drug users lost in the hell of addiction.

As I surveyed the scenes in which I would have been a participant only a few months before, I knew that I'd never be tempted by drugs again. The plight of the addicts was so hellish that I could only thank the Lord that I was no longer one of them. Never again would I succumb to the desire to shoot dope. Never!

Though I was certain enough of this, my brothers and sisters in Christ were less sure of me and, in my old surroundings, eyed me suspiciously. I realized they were only concerned for my welfare and yet their suspicions aroused anger in me.

In the meantime, back on Clinton Avenue, the atmosphere had become even more aggravating, for it was obvious that most of the associates on the Teen Challenge regarded my salvation from drugs as temporary.

When I'd first gone to Teen Challenge, I'd been the only girl at the Clinton Avenue residence which made my rehabilitation unusually difficult since the guys there, who were ex-addicts, held women addicts in special contempt. Having been on the streets themselves, they knew how a woman on the streets had to support her habit, to what depths she had to sink to pay for her dope. And most of them held that a woman with such a past was beyond help.

Apparently confirming this viewpoint, the girls' residence at Rhinebeck was finally closed on the pretext that it was going to be converted into a Bible School. But I felt that the real reason the girls had been sent away was that they simply hadn't responded to the rehabilitation program. Not as well as the men.

At the time I became a junior staff member, I was the only girl who'd been cured of her bad habits through Teen Challenge, so it wasn't surprising that some of my co-workers viewed my cure with skepticism.

However, the fact remained, I was off drugs for good. I was committed to Christ. So the skepticism of my colleges hurt and angered me.

I was so hurt, in fact, that one night I ran away from them and the shelter of Teen Challenge. It was a foolish thing to do but I'd been goaded into unreason by a male ex-addict who seemed certain that no woman junkie could be saved, physically or spiritually. He'd made his attitude so clear for days—even weeks—before I finally turned on him, telling him what I thought of him, and fled from the Clinton Avenue building.

Ruth saw me go and ran after me, vainly calling me to come back. I was so afraid she'd fall and hurt herself that I went back just long enough to return with her to the building. But then I left again and took a subway to freedom from the Teen Challenge atmosphere.

At the first stop, I got off and, finding a convenient park, sat on a bench trying to decide what Jesus would have done in my situation. For five hours I sat—but not alone. A junkie I knew had seen me and he joined me.

"They don't trust me," I complained to my sympathetic but glassy-eyed friend. "They claim they love the Lord at Teen Challenge but they sure don't act like it."

Then on and on I went, cataloguing my grievances against the organization which had done so much for me.

Stoned though he was, my junkie acquaintance

was attentive and full of advice. "Then just cut out of there," he urged. "You aren't having any fun with those people. If they don't trust you, just show them what you think of them by staying away.

"Come on with me. I'll take you back to the action. I can show you where to get some really good stuff.

"Come on. Let's go."

I thought of Christ standing on the mountain being tempted by Satan. The easy, instant pleasure available through a fix could be mine within the hour. Nobody would be judging me because I'd be back among people who were in no condition to judge.

Should I go back to the streets as some of my colleagues at Teen Challenge seemed so sure I'd do sooner or later?

Christ had been tempted by Satan, yes. But Christ had resisted the devil. The thought of the confrontation gripped me.

"No, man," I said. "I can't go with you. I got something I gotta do." And, so saying, I found a phone and called Ingrid.

"Cookie," she exclaimed with relief, "Where are you? Are you all right? We've been praying for you all evening. Please hurry. Please come home."

Prayers had protected me. But I'd had a close call. Terribly ashamed of what I'd done but terribly grateful for the faith of friends who'd asked God to shield me from the results of my own foolishness, I went back to Clinton Avenue.

"I was nearly lost again," I thought. "Thank you, Jesus, for saving me."

CHAPTER 21

New Sights, New People,
New Discouragement

During a midnight confrontation, Jesus had told me that He wanted me to work with young people and now, near the end of my first summer as a Teen Challenge junior counselor, I thought He was telling me something else. Though His voice wasn't as clear as it had been at our midnight meeting, I felt certain that He was speaking to me, calling me to go to a Bible college so that I'd be better prepared for the labors ahead.

I was a tenth grade dropout. I'd failed algebra. Yet, because I thought I was acting upon instructions from the Lord, I felt competent to attend a Bible school.

Dave Wilkerson, however, was less convinced about my leading.

"Cookie," he advised, "I'm not sure this is what the Lord wants you to do. Or at least I'm not sure that He wants you to go to Bible School just now.

"You're such a new Christian. You haven't even finished our full rehabilitation program. So I'm not sure you're ready for the pressures of Bible college, even if we had the money to send you.

A school will open at Rhinebeck soon. So why don't you wait and go there? We'll certainly make a place for you."

That was the sensible position Dave took, but, oddly, my good friend Ingrid agreed with me that God was pushing me out of Teen Challenge and into a learning experience. She was so sure, in fact, that she said she'd take me to her home in Colorado and help me raise money there to pay expenses at a Spanish American Bible College in El Paso which Nicky Cruz had told me about.

However, neither of us wanted to go to Colorado without discussing the matter further with Dave, so I approached him again.

"Dave, I still think Jesus is leading me toward Bible School," I told him, wondering whether my stubborn insistence might make him angry. "I really believe I should go."

Shaking his head in uncertainty, Dave said, "Well, Cookie, I know that the Spirit leads people in ways the human mind can't understand. So let's ask the Lord for a sure sign that will leave no doubt as to what you should do.

"If someone calls between now and next Thursday when Ingrid is leaving for Colorado and offers to sponsor you in Bible School for a year, I'll know that God wants you to go. If that doesn't happen, I hope you'll feel convinced that you're supposed to stay with us a while longer."

Meekly I agreed to accept the outcome of the test, although I felt it was unfair.

"Since nobody even knows that I want to go to Bible School, there's no way anyone will offer to send me," I told myself. My meekness was a facade. Inwardly, I was angry.

Dave and I reached our accord on Wednesday, so

the offer of sponsorship had to come within the next six and a half days, or I wouldn't get to go to college that fall. The time seemed entirely too short for such an offer to become possible.

But just two days after Dave had asked God for a sign, the couple who had chauffeured One-Eye Dutch and me to Teen Challenge a few months before, called to say they thought I should go to Bible College and that they would sponsor me.

Amazing! Yet no more amazing than all the other things that had happened to me in the immediate past. Imagine my excitement as I prepared to leave Brooklyn for my new adventure!

Except for the time I'd gone to the Kathryn Kuhlman meeting in Pennsylvania, I'd never left New York state, and the vast territory west of the Mississippi River sounded as exotic to me as Outer Mongolia.

The Lord had confirmed my leading that I was supposed to go to Bible School. God would take care of me, I knew, in the strange locales among the strange people I was about to encounter.

In August, Ingrid and I went to Denver where her brother-in-law was a minister at a Full Gospel church. I was traveling mostly on faith because, at that point, I had only ten dollars to my name and two changes of clothing.

Further, I shortly learned that my promised sponsors had been forced to withdraw their pledge of financial help because of an unexpected crisis in their own affairs. However, by this time, I'd discovered that the the Lord was going to provide one way or another, because, in Denver, church after church had asked Ingrid and me to share with their congregations our experiences with Teen Challenge. And the resulting contributions were enough to pay my college tuition for a year.

Although my years as a junkie had erased my prejudice against blacks, I'd arrived in Colorado with a prejudice against Caucasians, because I thought they were patronizing toward Puerto Ricans.

Ruth, Sharon, Ingrid and Dave had given me more love than any people I'd known (other than poor Nina), more than most of my own family had given me, yet I hadn't been able to get rid of my resentment against their race. However, the time that I spent in Denver taught me how sinful my bigotry had been and how foolish it is to generalize. For the people I met in Colorado, Caucasian for the most part, enriched me in more ways than one. Their generous monetary contribution toward my education made college possible, and their out-pouring of love made me strong enough to cope with what proved to be a disappointing, as well as unfamiliar, environment.

One of the Caucasians I met and learned to care for in Denver was a Baptist seminary student named Tom Robison who helped Ingrid and me get speaking engagements to which he often drove us. And though he and Ingrid weren't even dating, I was so impressed by him that I predicted he and my dear friend would marry within the year.

Ingrid was terribly embarrassed by my bold prophecy. But, to my delight, it came true.

Just before I was to go to school in El Paso, I got a call from Dave Wilkerson asking me to come to Pittsburgh at Teen Challenge expense, to tell my story before a youth rally there.

Sharon had sent me her trunk and some new clothes. Ingrid had given me a pair of new shoes, and congregations in and around Denver had given me money for my tuition, so I felt both confident and affluent when I flew out from Denver to Pittsburgh to address the youth rally.

Yet, as I stepped on the stage of the Syria Mosque, the very place in which I'd first encountered Jesus scarcely six months before, I felt only humble. Not proud. All the good things which had come to me— gifts of clothing, money and friendship and, above all, salvation—had come, not because I deserved them, but because God had blessed me far beyond my worth.

Jesus had made me a new creature. And as I stood on the stage where Dave and Kathryn Kuhlman had stood six months earlier, my happy heart cried, "Thank you, Lord," while tears rushed down my cheeks.

From Pittsburgh, I went to El Paso, to be met there by the Rev. Mr. Martinez, director of the Bible school I was to attend. When he introduced himself, I detected a hint of surprise in his face and voice and finally he confessed, "Cookie, you're not at all what we'd expected. I just don't believe it!"

What he'd expected, he never said, but since he'd been told that I was a former hard-fighting gang member and one of the roughest characters in the ghetto streets, he probably hadn't anticipated welcoming the 105-pound, conservatively dressed girl who'd stepped off the plane.

"Some young ladies are dying to meet you," Rev. Martinez continued as he introduced me to several girls who'd be sharing a dormitory with me. The girls were polite but looked as surprised as the school director had looked when we met.

Back at the school, while I settled into my dormitory room, girl after girl approached my door, introduced herself and then giggled insanely.

What, I wondered, was so hilarious about me?

Finally, one of the giggling girls explained. "It's just that you're not the way we thought you'd be at all. When we heard that you'd been a gang leader and a drug addict, we thought you'd be big and mean looking. But that's not how you are."

At that, I had to laugh too. There'd been a time when I looked mean, but I'd never been big. Yet, even as I laughed, I felt a pang. I was so different from the girls who were to be my classmates! Would I be considered an outcast here like I'd been so many times in my life?

I remembered the school I'd attended in Puerto Rico where, despite my good grades, I'd been shunned by the more affluent students. I remembered the first school I'd attended in New York and all the other places where I'd been too different to be accepted.

Was I going to suffer rejection again?

I had finally earned the acceptance in the slums by being meaner that the rest of my miserable peers. But that wouldn't be the way to win acceptance at Bible school.

A little chill ran over me as I finished unpacking. Maybe I had been a fool to come to this place.

Yet I still believed that Jesus had led me to El Paso and, since He'd led me, He was with me. So, thanking Him for His presence, I tried to put aside my fears.

CHAPTER 22

My First Real Christmas

Though I'd been in more depressing places (jails, for instance), the physical aspect of the Bible school was disappointing and dispiriting. I'd expected to be living and studying on a green campus dotted with dignified buildings, but the fact was far from that expectation.

Squat, ugly buildings were the color of dust on which they stood. As isolated from El Paso as the Rhinebeck hall for girls had been isolated from New York City, the campus was grim and uninspiring.

This would have disappointed me, but it wouldn't have depressed me so much had I quickly formed warm friendships with the other students. But this was impossible, for my background was so different from my classmates' that we couldn't find a common meeting ground. Young virgins, two or three years my junior, almost all of the girls had been strictly reared in Christian homes so that they knew absolutely nothing about life on the streets.

Further, though they all believed that Christ was the Son of God, not all had experienced a dramatic confrontation with Him.

As a result, it seemed to me that many had come to college more intent upon finding nice husbands than upon learning to serve Jesus more fully. My judgment was probably unfair, nevertheless, that's how it looked to me.

Thus, I was once again like a fish out of water, a misfit who didn't feel accepted by her peers, an unhappy outcast who only avoided feeling openly hostile because I knew that Jesus, at least, loved me.

That's how things went for a short while and then—boom!—something happened that very nearly shattered my control. I was asked to speak in chapel, a request which seemed simple to fill, since I'd been telling my story throughout the past summer on the streets of New York.

Always, when I was asked to face a crowd of strangers, I was nervous, but I thought that I should be less nervous than usual speaking to the Bible school students, because at least we knew each other, and they were familiar enough with my background to be partially prepared for what I would have to say.

Furthermore, the students were Christians (or so I'd been assured), so they would be receptive to my message. Or that's what I expected.

So I stepped to the platform with some confidence, less rattled by fear than usual.

Yet I'd spoken for only a minute or two when I heard a titter run through the audience. Then another. As I continued to speak, suppressed laughter broke out here and there in the crowd until it was hard for me to go on.

Still, I was sufficiently spurred on by God to finish my story, even though the suppressed giggles and furtive whispers hurt and distracted me.

After I'd finished speaking, nobody bothered to explain the curious reaction to my testimony. In fact, nobody spoke to me at all, except for the grammar teacher who said cryptically, "I think you'd better join my class."

For days I wondered what I'd done to provoke such titters, but gradually I realized that fellow students were making fun of my speech patterns whenever I spoke, privately as well as publicly, and I began to understand why they'd giggled during chapel.

My Spanish, which had been letterperfect when I was a child in Puerto Rico, had become a hybrid dialect picked up on the streets of the New York ghetto, and to my teachers and fellow students who spoke textbook Spanish it was embarrassing and funny.

If I'd been addressing a crowd in the Bronx slums, they would have found my language not only acceptable but entirely proper, for I was speaking in the slum-dweller's pigion lingo. But I wasn't speaking the language of the El Paso school's student body—in more ways than one!

Most of the teasing I got from classmates wasn't intended to be unkind, but I was too vulnerable not to be dreadfully hurt by it. As a matter of fact, I felt such a misfit that I began to wonder whether the Lord had actually directed me to come to the school and, recurringly, I thought of dropping out.

Maybe I should escape to New York, I thought, where people understand me—dialect, background and all. I needed friends in Texas but had none. I needed almost more self-discipline than I possessed to master the difficult curriculum and to abide by the endless rules which bound me on every side.

"I shall make you free," Christ had said but, at Bible School, I found myself a prisoner of a legion of restrictions which seemed senseless to me.

In order to strengthen myself to meet the school's demands, I sought a closer contact with the Lord through increased prayer time and, eventually, through fasting. I knew that some of the counselors at Teen Challenge had fasted when they needed extra spiritual strength and, though I didn't understand how fasting helped them, I decided to try it. So I set aside Wednesday as a day to forego food.

Unfortunately, from the human standpoint, I discovered only after I'd made Wednesday a fast day that Wednesday was the only day of the week when the school menu included meat—real meat, not just the scraps found in chili. But having made my pledge to the Lord that I wouldn't eat on that particular day, I bravely stuck to my resolution and, as a result, spent a mostly meatless school year.

Miraculously, though, I quickly began to enjoy the fruits of my fasting.

I'd never finished high school and, for eight years, I'd scrambled my brains with drugs. Yet, thanks to the Holy Spirit, the more I fasted and prayed, the more easily I was able to absorb such complicated subjects as doctrinal theology and homiletics.

Therefore, praising Jesus, I continued to forego all food for the twenty-four hours beginning each Wednesday morning. My studies became easier while my communion with Jesus became deeper and more rewarding so that, even though I continued to be a social outcast, my first months at school were profitable.

Yet I was still homesick. I missed New York and Dondi. I missed Sharon and Ingrid who wrote regularly but whose letters made me miss them all the more. And I missed the fellowship I'd shared at Teen Challenge.

Then, as Christmas approached, my homesickness increased. I didn't have enough money to go back to New York for the holidays, so all I could look forward to was lonely season in the dormitory, deserted by other students who were going home to their families—provided I could stay at the school at all. Since it was going to be completely closed for Christmas, it was doubtful that I could even stay in my room. So my holiday prospects were indeed discouraging.

However, just two weeks before the vacation was to begin, I got a wonderful present from Ingrid— bus fare to Denver, plus a letter inviting me to spend Christmas with her family.

I'd never spent Christmas with a real family before, unless Nina and I qualified as one when I was a child in Puerto Rico. So it was with apprehension and excitement that I left El Paso for Colorado.

Would I feel like an imposter, I wondered. Though Ingrid was wonderfully loving toward me, would her family be equally so? Would conservative Christians from the Middle West be able to welcome sincerely a former prostitute -junkie from the ghetto? And what would Ingrid's parents think if they knew about the Christmas eve I'd spent with the madman in New York who tortured and threatened me until I'd run naked and bleeding into the morning snow?

When Ingrid met me in Denver, her smiling cry of "Praise the Lord" temporarily eased my fears so that I was able to smile back as I, too, praised our Savior.

And when I met her parents at their home in South Dakota, my qualms were forever banished, for they welcomed me like a second daughter.

The entire Thatcher clan gathered for Christmas dinner which was a feast of love as well as of all the good foods traditional to the holiday. The love was like a balm, warming and comforting me and healing all the hurts I'd suffered in El Paso.

Then, when Christmas presents were distributed I, too, received a gift from every member of the family adding to my assurance that the Thatchers had truly received me as one of their own.

Later, as we all sang carols, I knew that I'd never been happier. I had asked Jesus to change my life and, oh, how wonderfully He'd complied. He'd saved my body from drugs and prostitution, my mind from madness and my soul for Eternity.

At the realization of all that He'd done for me, I left the family circle and fled to my room. There, alone except for my Lord, I cried even harder than I'd cried at the Kuhlman meeting in Pittsburgh.

CHAPTER 23

Cupid Takes Aim

In the way that a sleeping bear lives on his accumulated fat during the months of hibernation, I was going to have to live for the next several months on the love I'd received from the Thatchers.

Because, back at school, I was still an unhappy outcast. And, worse, I soon became involved in a new and unpleasant situation which added to my misery.

News that a former junkie-prostitute who'd been redeemed through Teen Challenge was in the neighborhood had spread through El Paso and its suburbs, and numbers of church congregations wanted to know more about me. As a result, I began to get invitations to tell my story in and around the city.

To add to my testimony, I asked three girls who sang well to go with me on my speaking engagements and treat the audience to some gospel music. The girls were very talented and worked out some nice arrangements which our listeners always enjoyed.

However, it soon became apparent that certain members of the school faculty weren't enjoying our popularity for, instead of encouraging us to go out and witness for the Lord, they began to throw roadblocks in our way. They resented the fact that I, who'd led a wicked, sordid life for years, was being invited to speak while they, who'd always tried to be good Christians, were being ignored. So, with increasing frequency, they scheduled special school activities on the nights when the trio and I had been invited to take our message to outside groups.

The reaction was human. It's hard to hear applause for a person when you don't think that person deserves it.

And my reaction was human, too. For instead of trying to maintain a charitable attitude toward the faculty members who were being less than charitable toward me, I grew, first, resentful and then stormily angry.

Never blessed with a mild disposition, I let my hair trigger temper explode one night with such force that it almost blew me out of the Bible school.

The girls who sang with me and I were about ready to walk off the campus enroute to an engagement when we were brought up short by the news that a special school event had been called.

I was furious. How dare these hypocrites do this to me, I complained to myself. How dare they?

Never considering that, if God had really wanted me to testify that night, He would have made the way easy, I stomped to my room, determined to pack up my few possessions and leave the school forever. No one was going to treat me so shabbily in the future!

Had my faith been older and steadier, I would have trusted the Lord to lead me into the places where He could use me best, but I was a relatively new, immature Christian who was still crawling rather than walking with God. So I packed and went as far as El Paso where I stopped at the home of a friend.

Here the Lord finally got my attention, reminding me during a night of prayer that I'd behaved like a spoiled child, more concerned with my own pride than with pleasing Him. For a long weekend, my Heavenly Father chided me for my pride and easy anger.

I recognized and was penitent for my faults. I told God that I was sorry for them. Yet it remained hard for me to go back to the school and say the same thing to the faculty members who'd offended me. Nevertheless I took a bus back.

Approaching the campus, I remembered the day I'd gone back to Teen Challenge after running away, and the memory of how I'd been welcomed gave me the courage I needed to walk back into the dormitory.

To my amazement, the Rev. Mr. Martinez greeted me as warmly and affectionately as the Teen Challenge staff had done when I'd returned to them after running away.

And from that time on, my attitude toward the college improved. In fact, I began giving the school a tenth of my offerings that I received when I spoke at churches and once, upon receiving the generous amount of $200, I gave it all to Rev. Martinez to buy a badly needed door for the dining hall.

The second semester went much better than the first had gone, for I was learning more easily, both in and out of the class. I found, to my pleasure, that I was not only mastering the complicated required courses, but I was learning to get along with others who, in turn, were learning to get along with me. And, while I never did form close friendships on the campus like my friendships with Sharon and Ingrid, I did come to feel accepted by the other students.

Finally I finished the year with (how amazing!) the

highest grades of any girl in school and the second highest in the entire student body. Despite the damage I'd done my brain through my long use of drugs, Christ had put it back into working order. When, in keeping with His promise, He made a new creature of me, He hadn't failed to renew my mind.

I hadn't enough money to get back home but, by speaking at churches along the way, I financed a bus trip to Chattanooga and, from there, I could afford to fly to New York.

However, as eager as I was to see Dondi, I didn't go directly to him but made a detour through Denver where I was a bridesmaid at a wedding I'd predicted. Ingrid, who'd been so flustered a few months before when I said that she'd marry Tom Robison, made my prophecy come true—to my great satisfaction.

I was thrilled that she married Tom, not because I'd said she would, but because I thought he was worthy of her. And few young men are of higher caliber!

Standing beside Ingrid during the ceremony, sensing the bridal couple's tremendous joy, I wasn't jealous, only glad for them. I didn't wonder whether I'd ever know the kind of romantic love my friends had found, because I was certain that I wouldn't, so certain that I didn't even think about it.

Because of the terrible experiences I'd had with men while I was a prostitute, I'd never felt physically attracted to one (except briefly to Dondi's father). I'd learned to love some men as my brothers in Christ, but none (Dondi's father included) had ever made my heart flutter foolishly, the blood rush to my cheeks, and my knees grow weak.

I'd seen Ingrid literally sparkle in Tom's presence, her love for him glowing and giving off a radiance that all could see. I'd seen her stammer and blush and act foolishly feminine because she loved him so much.

But I'd never met a man who affected me so.

Ah, well, I told myself, in the short year and three months that I'd been a Christian, I'd already been given a wealth of blessings. My Lord had been more than generous with His gifts. Romantic love was something I didn't need because, in the first place, I couldn't imagine any man loving me after he found out about my past and, besides, if I were mooning over some fellow, I might not be as free to work for Jesus.

In Ingrid's case, her love for Tom actually gave her more opportunity to serve the Lord, because her bridegroom was a preacher and, as a preacher's wife, she'd find her opportunities for service enlarged.

But as for me? Well, I thought, as Ingrid and Tom said their "I do's," I'm grateful for all that God's done for me already. It's more than enough.

However, God had even more startling blessings in store!

When I got back to New York, I was met at the airport by a Teen Challenge staff member who took me to Clinton Avenue headquarters where I was given a welcome piece of news. I learned that the Rev. John Benton and his family had moved into a building across the street from which they'd operate a rehabilitation program for women drug addicts and that they wanted me to become one of their counselors.

Naturally I accepted the invitation to work with this fine family because, for one thing, I had no home outside Teen Challenge but, more importantly, I believed that as a recent redeemed addict I could genuinely help the girls who were still on drugs.

My new job was a blessing in itself but another,

even more exciting one, was in store for I'd scarcely
started my career as a counselor before—wonder of
all wonders!—Dondi came to stay with me.

At first, Nina didn't think much of the suggestion.
She still wasn't so sure that I was a fit mother. Finally
though, since she was living on welfare and was
having trouble surviving at all and since it would be
easier for her to work if she didn't have Dondi to care
for, she sent him to me for the summer.

While I was at school, the State of New York had
at long last given me custody of my child, but the
gesture didn't mean much unless I could make a
home for him. And, up to that point, I didn't even
have a home for myself, other than Teen Challenge.
How could I ever make a home for Dondi, I
wondered, as I looked at the handsome little boy who
was my child. He was no longer a baby but a sturdy
little fellow of six.

There weren't many years left in which I could
cuddle him, I thought. Somehow, some way, I
wanted to keep Dondi with me, but I couldn't ask
Teen Challenge to support us both indefinitely.

Would I have to send him back to Nina in the
ghetto? As I puzzled and prayed over this question, I
was comforted by the knowledge that so far Jesus had
lovingly met my needs in the ways that had proved
best for me and mine, so He'd handle this problem
too, in exactly the right way.

Nevertheless, everytime I looked at my son, I
flinched at the memory of the years we'd been
separated. Every hour we spent together was doubly
precious because we'd known so few of them.

Meanwhile, I'd found a new friend at Teen
Challenge. But unlike Sharon and Ingrid and Ruth,
this one was a man.

His name was Demi Rodriquez and like me, he

was an ex-addict and a junior member of the staff.

As I've mentioned before, most male ex-addicts at Teen Challenge had a contempt for women who were former junkies which they couldn't seem to get out of their systems. Though they all knew the story of how Christ forgave and raised up the woman caught in adultery, and they knew Jesus had forgiven them, they weren't quite able to forgive women from the streets of their pasts. The guys may have supported their habits by muggings which they now admitted were sins but their manner seemed to say that women who'd supported their habits through prostitution had sinned more deeply.

If one of these men had been asked point blank, "Is it harder for Christ to forgive one of these women than for Him to forgive you?" he would have said. "no." And yet, by their attitudes, these same men who'd been junkies continued to condemn their newly redeemed sisters.

Demi Rodriguez, however, was different.

I was attracted by his dark good looks, but I was even more strongly attracted by his personality. There was nothing accusing in his manner, not even anything questioning.

He accepted me for what I was, a new creature, made new by the Lord. Whatever I'd been didn't concern him, for he really and truly believed that Jesus washed sins as white as snow.

So Demi treated me, not with poorly concealed suspicion, but with a friendly courtesy. He was as gallant toward me as he was toward the sheltered young volunteers from the Middle West who came to Teen Challenge with their ideals and virginity intact.

According to Teen Challenge rules, counselors weren't allowed to date each other, but I found myself watching for Demi in the halls, on the sidewalk, around and in the Teen Challenge buildings.

I wasn't yet hoping to experience romantic love, but I was certainly experiencing something unusual.

For one day I had to admit to myself that my heart was fluttering foolishly when Demi was near. Just as Ingrid's had done around Tom. I felt bubbly but strangely weak.

The likelihood of a tough cookie like Cookie blushing was remote enough to be laughable. Yet I even imagined that my cheeks were turning pink when Demi spoke to me.

Surely they weren't. Or were they?

Demi Rodriguez

CHAPTER 24

Times of Desperate Trial

"Cookie, come outside. There's been an accident."

I was in the chapel with some of the Teen Challenge staff when I heard the cry.

An accident? At first the word "accident" hardly registered. I'd been so happy during the past few weeks, working, worshipping and spending time with my child and with my new friend, Demi, that I was still vulnerable to disaster. Bad things just didn't happen to me anymore, praise God!

But as I ran out the chapel door in answer to the call, I broke out of euphoria.

An accident? Where was Dondi?

Dondi! That was it. Something must have happened to him.

And it had, for there he lay in the street, bleeding, curiously contorted, crying, "Mommy. Mommy."

During the weeks he'd spent with me, he'd been as healthy and happy as any little boy could be. He was petted by adults and welcomed as a playmate by young Jimmy Benton. Everyone seemed to love him and, in return, he loved the world. What a dear little boy he was. What a pleasure he'd been to me.

But now, perhaps, I was going to lose him. He'd been hit by a car and was badly hurt.

Rushing to my baby, I began to pray, "Dear Jesus, don't let Dondi die. Please save him. Please don't let him die." As I knelt beside him, weeping and praying, Don and Dave Wilkerson joined me, blending their prayers with mine.

As we placed our hands on Dondi, I remembered the Lord's promise, "When two or three are gathered together in my name. . . "

Jesus didn't lie, and He'd promised, when two or three are gathered together in faith, their prayers will be answered. "Please, Jesus," the three of us begged, "please save this child."

And remembering Christ's pledge, I was comforted. He'd promised, and His word was good, so I mustn't be afraid. I remembered that Jesus had taken care of my baby for me during the years when I wasn't fit to do it, so I was certain that He was going to take care of him now. I stopped crying. I was calm.

During the ambulance ride to the hospital, Dondi quit breathing but, even during that crisis as paramedics gave him artificial resuscitation, I was confident that he was going to be all right. Jesus had promised. The Lord's word was good.

At the hospital he was rushed into surgery where doctors set a compound fracture on his leg and treated his other injuries. His doctors told me what I already knew, that he was going to be all right. But I wasn't so sure that Nina would be.

She'd been reluctant to let me keep him in the first place, and I was pretty sure she'd consider the accident solid proof that I still wasn't a fit mother. I was afraid she'd decide that Teen Challenge was no place for Dondi and, reluctantly, I had to admit to myself that this might be the case. Could I work with street people and addicts and, at the same time, give enough attention to my son? I debated.

What was Nina going to say to me? And how should I answer her? I braced myself for a storm that I was certain would break.

However, Nina's reaction to the accident was the one thing I needn't have worried about, for God, using Demi Rodriguez as His instrument, had given her a calm acceptance of the near tragedy.

Dondi had scarcely been hit by the car and rushed to the hospital before Demi, led undoubtedly by the Holy Spirit, had taken the Teen Challenge van, rounded up my relatives, Nina included, and brought them back to the Teen Challenge chapel where he urged them to pray together for Dondi's recovery. Even my mother whom I hadn't seen in years was herded into the chapel to pray for her grandson's survival!

Since my relatives were scarcely a religious group, most of them not even on speaking terms with one another, much less with God, Demi had to have heavenly help in getting them all together and to their knees.

However, that's what he was able to accomplish and, as a result, Nina coped with the crisis without raging at me or accusing me of neglecting her precious Dondi.

As soon as I was sure that my baby was out of danger, I agreed to go back to Teen Challenge and to the work I'd been called to do. Demi, with a group of Gospel singers called the Collegians, came by the hospital to take me "home."

I wasn't aware of it when I climbed into the van, but the romantic-minded Collegians (having noticed that Demi and I were attracted to each other) had ordered him to let them out and take me to China-town for dinner. And, though he and I both knew that staff members weren't supposed to date, he went along with the plan.

After all, I supposed we both were reasoning, the circumstances were most unusual. I'd been through an emotionally and physically exhausting time, so a relaxing dinner away from both the hospital and the pressures of Teen Challenge might be good for me.

In any case, Demi and I went unchaperoned to a Chinese restaurant where we quickly found our-selves having a gloriously good time. We had so much in common, not only our Spanish heritage and our experience as addicts, but our deep faith in the Lord who'd saved us each from the drug-users hell.

During the evening, I may not have been as giggly as a schoolgirl. But, in many ways, I felt like one, for through being with Demi, I was pulsing with emotions most girls feel at sixteen but which I'd never felt before.

And because my emotions were so new, my body felt new too. With this man who treated me so gallantly, so considerately, I could momentarily forget the men who had mishandled me in the past.

Was I falling in love? The possibility was so pronounced that I finally had to face the question. Yet, I tried to assure myself, the answer to it was "No."

Two ex-junkies had no business falling in love! I tried to hold on to the idea.

Yes, I did believe that Christ's blood had washed our sins away, but even though we could now go to heaven, we shouldn't expect to find heaven on earth through human, earthly love.

The Son of God could love me as His redeemed child but surely no mortal man could be forgiving and loving enough to want me for his life's companion. Unthinkable!

Yet Demi did seem to forgive me and love me just as I unquestionably was falling in love with him. Still, after our dinner at the Chinese restaurant, we didn't try to date, because we knew that dating would violate Teen Challenge rules, and neither of us wanted to do anything dishonorable.

Our work brought us together with some regularity, though. For example, Demi drove the bus which took Spanish-speaking girls to church, so I was with him each Sunday while, throughout the remainder of the week, we consciously and unconsciously found ways to be with each other.

When finally other members of the Teen Challenge staff noticed our attachment, since all the world loves a lover, they were more pleased than displeased. Dave Wilkerson even gave Demi and me occasional permission to go out for Pizza together and once let us double date with my former counselor, Sharon and her fiance.

Thus our curious romance continued for some time until one afternoon Dave unexpectedly accosted Demi in the hall. "Demi," he said, "I want you and Cookie to be in my office at nine o'clock in the morning."

That was all. No clue as to what he wanted with us. But Demi and I shared a frightening suspicion that he was going to say something to us about our relationship.

That night Demi and I prayed together and the next morning, before going to see Dave, we did the same thing, begging Jesus to give us strength and wisdom.

Promptly at 9:00 a.m., we stood confronting Dave

who said nothing to us at first but, instead addressed our Lord.

"Jesus," he prayed, "Thank you for Demi; Thank you for Cookie. Thank you for the great love you have for them and for the deliverance you have given them. Continue to protect them and to bless them. Amen."

Then, gazing piercingly at me, he demanded, "Are you in love with Demi?"

Startled by his question, I reacted without thinking what the proper modest reaction should be. Not even stopping to wonder one more time whether Demi loved me, I simply allowed my heart to blurt out the single word my lips were forming, "Yes!"

Then, after hearing my own voice, I was overcome with embarrassment. How dared I declare my love for a man who might not want it but who'd be too much of a gentleman to reject me bluntly?

However, Dave didn't give me time to regret my boldness for long.

"Demi," he inquired, "Do you love Cookie?"

And, joy of joys, Demi answered even more quickly than I had, "Yes," he said, "I do. I do love Cookie."

"Then, Cookie," Dave wanted to know, "If Demi gave you an engagement ring, would you accept it?"

"Yes," very softly but very certainly I said that I would.

"And, Demi," Dave went on, "would you like to give Cookie an engagement ring?"

Demi replied that he'd like to.

"All right," Dave concluded matter of factly, "here's $25 for the down payment. I'll sign for you to pay the rest on terms.

"Now go get the ring."

Becoming engaged to Demi had turned out to be

quite simple, thanks to Dave Wilkerson's no-nonsense approach. However, getting married was another matter altogether.

First and foremost, I had a problem with conscience, of which no one except myself and my Lord was aware.

As a prostitute, I'd learned that most prostitutes use various birth control devices to avoid pregancy. Yet I never had. And I'd only been pregnant one time. With Dondi.

This must mean, I thought, that my body had been so abused I could no longer conceive a child. Though I'd never asked a doctor about this, such was the conclusion I'd drawn.

That being the case, if I loved Demi (and, oh, how I loved him!), could I be so unfair as to marry him and deny him the children he'd surely want? Should I reveal my fears to him and risk losing him? If I did tell him, would he still want me, in spite of all the handicaps?

I thought I knew the answers to the first two questions but not to the last, and it was uncertainty about the last answer which froze my heart and my lips. So chilled by the realization that I might lose this man, I simply could not mouth the words conscience told me say.

I couldn't force myself to warn him that I might be a critically impaired wife, incapable of giving him sons and daughters.

I also worried lest I couldn't give him the physical response a wife should give her husband. My past contacts with men had been more nearly revolting than thrilling, so I wasn't sure that I could thrill to a bridegroom's ardor.

Suppose that, on my wedding night, the memory of every indignity I'd ever suffered through men traumatized me. How awful that would be for Demi! How tragic!

Yet I loved him deeply.

Finally, I wondered, how would marriage affect my work for Jesus? I'd been accepted by a Bible college in Minneapolis which expected me to enroll in the fall, and I felt it my duty to continue my education.

Since there was no way I could plunge whole-heartedly into matrimony and another year of college in an out-of-town school at the same time, I was confronted with a heartbreaking choice.

If I got married right away, I'd have to cut short the education which I believed I needed to serve God more fully. On the other hand, if I went away to school, I'd have to postpone marriage for at least a year.

What should I do? I prayed hard, yet I got no clear answer. So finally I returned my engagement ring to Demi.

CHAPTER 25

We're Married

I returned the ring to Demi; he returned it to me. This went on until the ring had passed back and forth at least three times, while Nina looked on aghast.

She was one hundred percent in favor of my marriage to Demi which couldn't take place soon enough to suit her. She may have wondered how I'd qualified to catch such a good man, but she was sure that Demi was exactly what I needed to keep me on the straight and narrow path. With him, she declared, I'd settle down.

Without him? Well. . . despite the evidence that I'd completely reformed, Nina still had doubts about my stability.

Meanwhile I didn't so much as want to talk about a wedding, much less set a date, so Demi finally reluctantly agreed that maybe we should leave plans in abeyance.

I had sent a deposit to apply on my tuition at the school I planned to attend and accepted a series of speaking engagements in the midwest which would help pay my expenses.

Then, on the day before I was to leave New York,

Dave Wilkerson announced that he didn't think I should go. He'd been traveling quite a lot, therefore, hadn't had the chance to talk with me earlier. But, at the very last minute, he surprised me by declaring that he thought I shouldn't go off to school.

"What about Dondi?" he asked. "And Demi? You owe them something, you know. Are you sure you're not going back to school just to profit Cookie? Think carefully about your motives and about where you are really needed most.

I had to admit that I'd worried and prayed a lot about what I should do. But I hadn't gotten any clear answer from God and now my plans were so dim that I could scarcely change them.

I simply couldn't default on my speaking engagements, could I?

Nobody tried convincing me further to stay at Teen Challenge so, still confused, I began my tour.

The schedule proved exhausting, and I was more homesick than I'd been in El Paso, for now I missed Demi as well as Dondi. When I wasn't on a speaker's platform, I was on the long distance telephone talking with Demi, nourishing myself with the sound of his voice.

Finally, on the last night of my tour, I impulsively dialed Dave's number and was relieved to hear him tell me again, "Forget college, Cookie. Come back to us. You'll always have a place at Teen Challenge, and there are people here who need you."

There were also people there whom I needed, needed so desperately that I couldn't stay away from them any longer. So I hurried back to New York where I turned over the donations I'd collected through my talks to Teen Challenge to be applied toward the education of someone else.

Though Dave had promised there'd always be a

place for me at Teen Challenge, there really wasn't a place when I got back to New York. So I went back to the slums to spend some time with Nina and Dondi.

During the time I'd been away, I'd remembered the environment as bad, but it was even worse than my recollections. Dirt, profanity, obscenity everywhere. Men and women bawling at one another. . . children whining and crying. Drunks lying on the sidewalks and stairways.

Almost hourly the sights and sounds drove me to my knees to beg God to save these people who were forced to exist in such surroundings and to help me bring Dondi out of them.

In time, Teen Challenge found another job for me, not as a full-time counselor but as a clerk typist using the meager skills I'd acquired at the vocational high school. The job wasn't what I'd hoped for, but I welcomed it, because it gave me a chance to minister in the streets at night and to spend some time with Demi.

Well-meaning friends were nearly driving us crazy with their conflicting advice—"Marry at once. Avoid temptation."—"Don't do anything hasty. Don't marry unless you're sure of what you're doing." Consequently, we continued to postpone our wedding day though, as the weeks passed, Demi and I grew closer and closer.

In the streets, he was constantly reminded of my past, if he couldn't put it out of his mind completely, he outwardly ignored it. As much as anyone I'd ever met, he held to Jesus' injunction, "Let him who is without sin among you cast the first stone." With his whole heart, he accepted Christ's pledge that the most scarlet sins could be washed white as snow.

How dear he was! How deeply I loved and needed him! Yet I don't know when, if ever, we would have married had Dave Wilkerson not spoken out again. It was he who said, "Weigh all the evidence; listen to all the advice; and then go with God's leading, not the world's."

Well, this finally resolved my doubts about marrying Demi and his as to whether I was ready to be his wife. God had brought us together.

So, on December 10, 1966, we were married in the Manhattan church his parents attended. A white bridal gown didn't seem quite appropriate, so I wore a beige dress I'd bought with my very last penny.

Yet, in every other respect, I was a typical first-time bride, excited, flustered, a bundle of nerves. Sharon was my matron of honor, while her husband, Richard, was not only Demi's best man but the escort who squired me to the church.

Because I'd declined to ride to my wedding in the old Teen Challenge van, Richard came for me in his white automobile. However, after we'd climbed in, it refused to start, so I was chauffeured in the van after all. This was a disappointment, though one which was forgotten as soon as we reached the church.

There we were greeted by the Teen Challenge staff, by all of Demi's family and mine, including my mother and delighted grandmother. My mother looked so young and pretty that many people mistook us for sisters, while Nina—tough little Nina—for once in her life, was softly tender as she embraced me.

As we recited our vows, both Demi and I were strongly conscious that we were part of a triangle, for we'd invited Christ to be a part of our marriage, to be a permanent guest in our home.

At the reception at the church which followed the ceremony, many of the friends who wished us well pressed envelopes into our hands containing cash so that Demi and I were able to start our married life with $200. That's all we had, except our love for each other and the Lord. But with that we had quite enough.

It was fortunate that we had asked Jesus to be a party to our union because, if we hadn't had Him, we might not have had each other long.

Adjustments between a new husband and wife are always difficult. The mere fact that two people are two people instead of one guarantees that they'll have certain differences, and Demi and I had ours.

Sexually, we had no problems. My fears about my response to a bridegroom had been groundless, reminding me once again that Jesus not only forgives completely, He heals completely. When, through His grace, He creates a new, whole person, He does so without reservation.

However, because of our work and life, Demi and I had more adjustments to make than most newlyweds. In the first place, we traveled a great deal, functioning as a public relations team in advance of Dave's rallies held throughout New York state.

Further, Demi and I not only gave our testimonies at these rallies, but I was often presented as a sort of a showpiece, redeemed after extraordinary sins, and pretty soon this began to bother Demi.

I could understand why Dave liked to dwell on my past, for I was an exceptional representative of Jesus' redeeming power. I was the only female ex-junkie on the Teen Challenge staff and Dave found it effective to emphasize how despicable I'd been before Christ turned my life around.

I didn't mind his graphic descriptions of the person I used to be, for I knew that Cookie no longer existed, praise the Lord! But, while I didn't realize it, each sizzling phrase was making Demi flinch.

And one night he could stand no more. Immediately after the meeting he accosted Dave. "Look," he said, "I appreciate what you are trying to do. You are using Cookie as an example to show what life on the streets is like; how rotten a junkie's life can be.

"I know what Cookie's been through, but that's all over now, and I can't stand to hear you talk about my wife that way.

"If that has to be a part of your ministry, I'm afraid Cookie and I can't work with you anymore."

CHAPTER 26

We Try to Escape Our Past

Dave was as shocked as I at Demi's outburst. But he was also understanding. So right then and there, after praying with us, he decided that we should get out of the streets and go back to the Teen Challenge Center.

My surprise at my husband's protest was total and genuine because, until he'd reached his breaking point, he'd completely disguised the pain he felt when anyone flaunted my past.

I was surprised that Demi had suffered so much in silence, but happily amazed to find myself cherished and protected, since no one had ever cherished and protected me before. That took a little getting used to.

But, as I gradually came to comprehend that Demi loved me so much he wanted to be my buffer against everything in the world that could hurt me, against tormenting memories, against gossip, against every man-made evil, I loved him more than ever.

At the Center, Demi went to work as a counselor and was quickly promoted to assistant dean. But, since married women weren't allowed to be counselors, I could only serve as a clerk typist.

My work didn't place the strain on my time, strength and emotions that Demi's placed on his. He could scarcely find enough hours in each twenty-four to give to the boys under his care the help he knew they deserved. And he could find almost no time for me.

I understood his dedication to the addicts and ex-addicts who needed him, but I needed him too, so I began to resent his devotion to them. While Demi had too little free time, I had too much—including leisure hours in which to brood over the way I thought my bridegroom was neglecting me.

Compounding the resulting friction was the fact that we had almost as little privacy as a couple of goldfish. Our honeymoon love nest was one room in the Teen Challenge Center to which we could seldom retreat together.

The staff was not only conscious of our newlywed status but of our moods. And the knowledge that so many eyes were upon us only increased our edginess.

Since I had never been close to a happy marriage for more than an hour or so at a time, I didn't realize that even the happiest couples sometimes disagree—or fight—and even the most doting wife will find imperfection in her husband, just as I was beginning to notice a few in Demi.

Nor did I understand that a husband can occasionally criticize his wife without ceasing to love her.

As our bickering increased, I began to wonder what we'd done to offend Jesus, for He no longer seemed to be a part of our family circle.

Both Demi and I continued to pray diligently that we be led into a sweeter relationship and, before long, our prayers were answered—not with a leading but with a PUSH!

We were shoved right out of the Brooklyn Teen

Challenge Center and out of the circle of concerned friends, whose interest was about to destroy us, by the offer of a job in St. Louis. Teen Challenge was about to launch a rehabilitation program there, and Demi was invited to join the staff.

For more reasons than one, he jumped at the chance to change our surroundings.

We'd scarcely settled in St. Louis when, to our great joy, I discovered that I was pregnant. All my fears that I couldn't conceive had been unfounded.

The Lord's bounty was proving to be as endless as His mercy.

Demi loved Dondi as deeply as though he were his own son but, because of Nina's objections, we couldn't have him with us all the time and, even if we could, Demi and I wanted children born to the two of us to be Dondi's brothers and sisters.

Since I'd been declared a fit mother, I could have wrenched Dondi away from Nina but she'd taken him when he was a scrawny, ailing infant, unwanted by his parents, and had nursed him into healthy childhood.

She loved him frantically, so I didn't have the heart to tear him away from her entirely.

Before we left Brooklyn, Nina had allowed Dondi to visit us on weekends and, after our move, she allowed him to spend a summer in St. Louis. However, she wouldn't consider turning him over to us permanently.

Demi wanted to adopt Dondi, yet he and I both knew that he had only the slimmest chance of being approved as an adoptive father. Both he and I were ex-junkies and, on top of that, he didn't have what the world would call a steady job. Teen Challenge had no regular income and neither did its staff members. It operated through donations which came in answer to prayer. And being on the staff of such an organization scarcely made Demi financially responsible.

Maybe, Demi and I decided, the Lord wanted us to change our entire lifestyle. Maybe He wanted us to break out of the Teen Challenge cocoon and go out into the secular world.

We asked God to tell us what to do and, while He didn't answer through a bolt of lightning or some such dramatic display, we concluded that He did will that we become "civilians" or, at least He wouldn't object if we did.

So Demi resigned from the Teen Challenge staff and we moved to Columbus where friends helped us find an apartment and aided Demi in finding a job as a mechanic.

Just before we left St. Louis, God seemed to demonstrate His approval of what we were doing, surprising us with yet another blessing.

Nina called to say that, since New York teachers were on strike, we could take Dondi with us to Columbus and put him into school there.

Once in Columbus, we felt momentary twinges of conscience, remembering the work Teen Challenge was doing and that we could still be sharing in it. But as we became a part of the community, we resolved that we were in the place we were supposed to be.

In November our son, Danny was born, and soon afterward Nina called again, this time to say that we could keep Dondi—permanently.

What a happy family we were! Demi was making a good salary and, when a neighbor offered to babysit, I got a job, too, for it was important to us that we be able to prove to the court's satisfaction that we were a reliable, financially sound couple.

This we did so that, in the spring of 1969, Demi was able to adopt Dondi.

We were doing so well that we bought a home—a nice, brick house with three bedrooms and wall-to-wall carpeting. We had two cars and, with the birth of our daughter, Crissy, on December 10, 1969, we had three children.

Dondi's acceptance of Demi had moved a bit slower than Demi's acceptance of him. Though still a very small boy, he didn't want to share me with another male animal but, by the time of Crissy's birth, he had come to love Demi as a father, just as Demi gave him a father's love.

Now we were blissfully happy in Columbus except for one thing. We'd never told our neighbors about our pasts and we knew that, in keeping our secrets, we might be shortcoming our Savior. Our stories were so remarkable that, if we revealed them, we might lead others to salvation

Nevertheless, we rather cagily avoided revealing our sordid histories.

When I filled out an application for a job, I didn't lie, but neither did I tell all of the truth.

Thus, when asked to be a "block parent," I declined to serve rather than risk an investigation into my character and background.

Dondi was heartbroken when his Mom said she couldn't hold the neighborhood office, but I was afraid of repercussions if I accepted it.

Finally Demi and I told a few close friends about the shameful lives from which Jesus had rescued us. Generally speaking, however, we maintained very low profiles, trying to assure ourselves that, by sharing our stories in this limited way, we were doing our best for Jesus. Yet we continued to be nagged by our consciences.

Shouldn't we perhaps broadcast our testimonies? Shouldn't we tell the world how we knew from personal experience that Jesus could take the dregs of humanity and, from such poor clay, make a nice, respectable Columbus couple with a three-bedroom, brick bungalow?

From a worldly point of view, Demi and I possessed everything to make us happy—financial security, precious children, friends and our love for each other, for our marital adjustment was finally complete. And I would say that we were divinely happy except that our bliss was marred by a faint, divine nudging.

Just as we believed that God had led us to Columbus, we were now beginning to get the feeling that He was going to lead us away from it.

By being a decent, middle class couple we weren't doing anything overtly wrong, and yet, we had to ask ourselves, how about our sins of omission? Complacency would offend God. We must not place our security and popularity above our duty to our Savior.

At about the time Crissy was born, we began to see on television and read in the papers more and more about the spread of drug addiction. It was no longer confined to the ghettos but had become the curse of the college campus, of rural communities, and even of grammar schools. Demi and I prayed a lot about this because we, above all people, knew how drugs could destroy lives.

But praying was all we did to help stop the spread of addiction, until we saw a television special one night which literally sickened us. For it cited the case of a twelve-year-old who'd died from an overdose of heroin.

Twelve years old! Not even I had been on drugs at that age.

Dondi was almost ten and, from my point of view, still a baby. How was it possible that a child only two years older than he should O.D. on heroin?

Thoroughly shaken by the show, Demi said, "Let's pray together about this." When we arose from our knees, we knew that our comfortable, suburban life might be over, for both of us felt strongly that the Lord might be asking us to go back to the ghetto to help save His lambs.

The following Monday morning Demi called Dave and talked with him about the Teen Challenge program, its current progress and problems. Then he flew to New York to talk with Dave some more, while I stayed in Columbus talking to God.

"Lord," I asked over and over, "please show us clearly what you want us to do."

I had quit work when Crissy was born, now that Demi was supporting us quite adequately, because I wanted to spend full time with my children. Making a home for my husband and our little people was fulfilling work, joyous work. And I knew that, if I went back into the ghetto streets to work with addicts, I'd have much less time for my own family.

What should I do? The question was a heart-wrenching one.

"Jesus," I begged, "please answer me. Will I be sacrificing my own children for the sake of others if I work full-time for you?"

"I took care of Dondi when you were working full time for me, didn't I?" the Lord replied. And I certainly couldn't argue with that logic.

So, after Demi returned from New York and we'd talked and prayed together some more, we decided to sell our house and go back to the New York slums.

On June 5, 1970, we rejoined Teen Challenge. Demi immediately resumed his duties as a counselor, while I was asked by Dave to direct a summer evangelism program.

The offer of this responsibility was both flattering and surprising, due to the fact no woman had ever directed the Teen Challenge street evangelism campaign.

Since Dave had said he'd find a reliable babysitter for me, I accepted the opportunity enthusiastically and was soon back in the streets holding rallies and urging junkies to give their lives to God.

Teen Challenge's income had improved substantially during our stay in Columbus so that Demi and I were paid almost regularly and were able to afford a small apartment.

Since junkies are night people, I instituted a series of night rallies to which crowds were drawn initially to escape the discomforts of the hot tenement buildings. But soon they'd begin to clap to our gospel music and eventually a few would respond to our promise that Jesus loved them.

As his schedule allowed, Demi spoke at the rallies I organized. But, whether we were testifying together or apart, we found a great personal peace through our efforts in knowing that we were trying to do our best for Jesus. We could never pay Him all that we owed Him, but at least we weren't being indifferent debtors.

Then one night at a rally I met a girl named Frances and, through her, Demi and I learned how we could do something new and freshly exciting for the Lord.

CHAPTER 27

Back to the Streets and Jail

Frances was a junkie who somehow reminded me of myself. When I first saw her at a rally in the Bronx, she wasn't at all enthusiastic. She'd retreated to the edge of the crowd where she stood gazing at the sidewalk.

Urged on by the Holy Spirit, I aimed my message directly at her and, after the meeting was over, I told her I'd be back the next day to talk with her some more. We set a time and place to meet, though I wasn't at all certain Frances would keep the appointment.

However, she was at the meeting place ahead of time, avid to hear more about our Lord. She'd been as bad as any girl on the street, yet she responded eagerly to the good news that Jesus could make her a new person.

Demi hadn't ministered to girls but he, too, became interested in Frances and often, when I hadn't planned to go to the Bronx, suggested that we visit her. Through her he began to see the great need for an expanded program to help women addicts. For the Teen Challenge program for women, as it existed then, was pitifully inadequate.

John Benton was still in charge of a women's rehabilitation center in Garrison, New York, but it could accomodate only a tragically small number of girls so that, all too often, after a female junkie decided she wanted to be saved, she could find no earthly place to go for help. While she was going to God in prayer, she needed a place to sleep, wholesome food, and friends to give her spiritual nourishment and add their corporate prayers to hers.

And Teen Challenge simply didn't have room for more than a handful of girls. Because facilities were so limited, the program accepted only the most promising applicants, and I realized that under the new conditions Teen Challenge would have rejected me.

As Demi and I continued to work with Frances (we couldn't get her into the Teen Challenge rehabilitation center), we thought of the hundreds and thousands of girls on the streets who needed our help. And we felt frustrated that we could do so little for them.

Meanwhile, I discovered that I was pregnant again, having made the discovery in a most unpleasant way.

I was chronically, violently nauseated, so sick that I had to give up my street ministry and help Teen Challenge, only occasionally, by babysitting for staff members.

However, in the fourth month of my pregnancy, I began to feel much better and I also began to get the idea that the Lord was calling me to work in a new field.

Jail.

Nauseated as I'd been, I hadn't been too sick to

pray and, in all my prayers, I'd asked the Lord to show me how I could help His lost daughters. He'd answered me twice with a vision of the women's detention house in Greenwich Village, a foul place where I myself had been a prisoner.

"I don't know what this means," I'd argued with God. "You surely don't want me to work there, because I could never get in unless I were arrested again. With my record, the authorities would never let me spend time with the inmates."

Still the impression persisted that I should minister to the women in the Greenwich Village prison.

Yet I continued to hedge a little.

"Lord," I said, "before I do this, I'll have to get John Benton and Don Wilkerson to approve. If I get their approval, I'll try to visit the women prisoners."

I thought this might delay my projected mission indefinitely because, with John stationed in Garrison, he was almost never at the Brooklyn center. However, when I went to Don's office that morning and asked to see him, I was informed he was inside with—of all people!—John.

Jesus had moved so fast to set me on my new course that I moved fast too. Bursting into the office, I told the two men what I wanted to do, and they, without missing a beat, said, "If the Lord is leading you, do it."

Then I remembered that I hadn't discussed my new idea with Demi who definitely didn't want me working while I was pregnant. Suppose he objected. What should I do then?

Demi was out of town, but when he called that night, I promptly told him I felt moved to testify to women in prison and, to my satisfaction, he concurred. "Go ahead. If that's what God is telling you to do, of course you must do it."

Now the way was clear for me to go into the Greenwich Village detention house except for one little thing, namely: I had no pass. And though Don had equipped me with a letter of recommendation, I doubted seriously that I'd get one. An ex-junkie-prostitute-shoplifter wasn't welcomed by authorities as a suitable associate for jailbirds.

In his letter, Don had mentioned that I was a rehabilitated addict and, to me, that seemed an unnecessary bit of information to pass along to the Department of Corrections.

I should have realized that, if Jesus wanted me to minister to women in prison, I'd get my pass regardless of what my earthly credentials were. But my faith wasn't strong enough to give me this confidence, so I dictated another letter which omitted mention of my former drug use and, with it in hand, trotted to the office of the Department of Corrections.

Then an officer took my self-dictated recommendation and studied it. His mask-like face told me nothing as he went over and over the letter. In fact, he was so non-committal for so long a time, I finally burst out, "I'm an ex-addict myself, but through Jesus I'm cured."

The official's face was still non-committal as he continued to study me.

"How long ago were you on drugs?" he asked. I had to count back through the years which had passed since I had my last fix.

"Seven." Seven years had gone by since One-Eye Dutch had dragged me to Teen Challenge, and Jesus released me forever from my habit.

When I told the officer that I'd been clean for seven years, he at last permitted himself a small show of emotion. He smiled.

"Well," he admitted, "then you are technically a

cured addict. The state has legislated that a person who's been off drugs for five years is cured, but not many make it, I hear. In fact I've never before met a woman who made it. Congratulations."

And with that, I got my permit.

I hadn't realized before that I was cured according to the laws of New York, but I knew that Jesus, according to His promises, had freed me from my habit. He'd promised to heal and save everyone who turned to Him, and I was living proof of His truth.

I'd thought that, with my pass, I could walk right into jail and minister to the girls confined there, but when I got to the detention facility, I was stopped by a cold-eyed matron who told me brusquely, "We have too many people coming in to talk with the inmates now. We can't accept anymore."

I was so shattered I didn't notice whether she said she was sorry, but I don't believe she did. The Lord had made my path so easy this far that I was stunned to find a stumbling block in a matron's uniform in my way.

And she hadn't even said, "Maybe some other time." She'd simply said, "No. No, you can't visit the inmates."

Well, at this stage I wasn't about to give up my mission without argument, so I proceeded to pour out my personal story, trying to make the matron see why I felt a special burden for the girls in her custody. I talked emotionally—wildly, maybe—for, as I recounted my past, the horror of it became vivid to me, while the joy of being snatched from it became just as vivid.

Finally I could see the matron's reserve breaking. She'd steeled herself against me but, as she'd listened to my story, she'd become interested in what I had to tell, very nearly convinced that I had something important to offer the women prisoners.

Then, at last, she was convinced. But she didn't relent entirely. "All right," she told me. "I'll let you talk with one girl for two hours once a week. That's all I can do."

And, so saying, she launched me into a work which would change not only my entire life but the lives of my husband and children.

CHAPTER 28

Curbside Beggar

Lois, the first girl I approached through my jail ministry, was allowed to meet me in the corner of the Social Services Department office.

We weren't able to talk confidentially, and with so many people working around us, it was hard to concentrate. Nevertheless, the Holy Spirit put words in my mouth which touched Lois enough to make her want to meet with me again the next week.

We met twice, then when she reported for our third encounter, Lois brought a friend. I use the term "friend" loosely, for the scowling, bitter girl who'd come to our conference didn't know what friendship meant. She was like I'd been when I was on the streets, too filled with suspicion and hostility to feel warmth toward anyone.

However, she said she'd come in Lois' interest, to show her that I was a fraud who'd been filling her with a pack of lies.

"Maybe," she added charitably, I was "just plain crazy."

She knew I was lying, she insisted, because I claimed that Jesus had taken me off hard drugs, adding "I've been on drugs for five years and I know there's no way out."

When I'd first seen this girl, Colleen, I'd actually been afraid. Her obvious, aggressive hatred for the world was frightening.

But as I heard her confess to the hopelessness of her addiction, my fear gave way to pity, for I remembered what it was like to be a junkie with no hope of escape from a junkie's hell.

Colleen was a nasty character, in jail for murder! She and her "live-in" boyfriend had only intended to hold up a grocery store, but when the grocer had drawn a knife, Colleen responded by shooting him. The boyfriend, meanwhile, had split... leaving her to pay for the crime alone.

This is what had embittered her most—that he had abandoned her.

"I'm alone," she said, "and that's how I want to be from now on. I'm not going to depend on anybody. Because you can't trust anybody to stand by you when you're really in trouble.

"Oh, no?" I thought. "Oh, no? What about Jesus?"

Since Colleen didn't know about Jesus, it was no wonder that she felt forsaken, for most of us have felt that way at one time or another, especially when we walk without the Lord.

"Colleen," I began, "there's one person you can depend on who'll help you anytime you call on Him and who'll love you no matter what you do.

"I know this is the truth, because He's stood by me."

Then I told her about my past, about the father who'd deserted me through suicide before I was born; about the mother who'd then given me away; about my grandmother who'd thought I was unredeemable, and about the kids at school who'd scorned me.

Then I told her of how I'd learned about Jesus; how He'd forgiven me everything and had made me a new creature.

"He's with me all the time," I added, "just as He's with you. And he loves us both."

By the time I'd finished speaking, Colleen was sobbing. "Oh, Cookie," she cried, "I've been so lonely and afraid. I do need Jesus. Please tell Him I want His love."

Together we prayed, and the Lord so changed Colleen that, even though she was sentenced to the penitentiary for seven years, she claimed she was actually free, because Jesus had released her addiction and her sins. And her testimony continues to lead other prisoners to freedom through Christ!

When the House of Detention was moved into new quarters on Riker's Island, I asked to be given more space and more time for counseling, but the situation became more difficult, if anything.

At first, in the new building, I could only talk with the inmates by telephone through a glass partition. Finally, though, the prison chaplain must have been impressed, either by my persistence or by the change my ministry was making in some of the girls, because he offered the use of his small office for Bible study.

Meanwhile, on a Tuesday, my baby, a little girl, was born. I'd been at the jail ministering the day before her birth and, on the next Monday, I was back again, proving that the Lord was not only supplying me with the right words to say but the strength to say them.

In time, so many girls were reporting for Bible study that the warden allocated an office and two classrooms for our use. Many of the prisoners who'd given themselves to Jesus received the baptism of the

Holy Spirit and soon were organizing evening prayer groups in their cells until eighteen such groups were meeting. Only the Lord Himself could have brought this about.

Though the prison ministry bore wonderful fruit, it sometimes drained me emotionally until I could scarcely carry on. Burdened by the horrible stories I heard from the girls, I'd become almost immobilized by depression until, through praying with Demi and my Christian friends, I'd gain relief and spiritual refreshment.

While the prison ministry was often a "downer," it was more often an "upper," serving as a thrilling adventure which brought new challenges and new victories every day. In time, it mushroomed beyond the walls of the House of Detention for, as girls became eligible for release (either through parole or because they'd served their sentences), I found myself more deeply involved with them than ever. Often I was their only friend in the outside world, so it was to me that they turned for, not just moral support, but actual shelter.

A new Christian who'd just come off drugs and was coming out of jail needed a half-way house, a place to which she could go for continuing rehabilitation and Christian love before she went into Society. Tragically, the only Christian home for girls was usually full to the rafters and couldn't make room for another applicant.

So, as the girls I'd counselled came out of prison, I could pray they'd continue walking with Jesus, but usually that was all I could do.

Demi, realizing how it upset me to watch new converts struggling to stay off the streets, tried to console me.

"Honey," he'd say, "just be glad that you've been

able to do as much for them as you've done. Thank God for what He's accomplished through your ministry because He's been using you in a glorious way.

"Some of these girls wouldn't want to be in a rehabilitation center even if there were one to take them. And you can only do so much, so praise God for the work He's given you to do."

I did praise God, of course, for I'd seen miracles at the prison, the miraculous cleansing of sins, the miraculous healing of tortured souls. Still, I couldn't help worrying about those women who'd been drug addicts for, more than Demi, I realized what their temptations were like.

Though Jesus said in defense of the woman taken in adultery, "Let him who is without sin among you cast the first stone," Society finds it very hard not to cast stones at the woman who's been on the streets. And because Society is so slow to forgive her, she, more than a man, finds it hard to appreciate fully the cleansing power of Jesus' blood.

More than a man, she needs prayer and under-standing, patience and spiritual support. Oh, how well I knew her needs! No one alive could know better than I.

So I fumed and fretted, weeping inwardly over the plight of the newly redeemed junkies who had nowhere to go except back to the gutters from whence they'd come.

One day I was in court with an addict named Rosita who'd been caught stealing (as usual) in order to support her habit and to survive.

She expected to go to jail (as usual) but the judge surprised her by announcing that he was going to parole her to a Christian program. Neither Rosita nor I could easily believe the good news. She'd fully expected to be locked up again, while I was painfully afraid that, if she went back to prison, she'd be lost forever.

Rosita had been reaching toward Christ, but her grip on faith was tenuous, and another term behind bars might destroy it and discourage her from ever reaching out again. So I was as happy as she when the judge turned her over to a Christian program.

Unfortunately, the only Christian centers for girls in the New York area were full to capacity (as usual), but I already had an alternative in mind.

"There's been a new center for girls opened in Puerto Rico," I told Rosita. "How would you like to go there? I'm sure there'd be a place for you."

She said that she'd like to go, that it would certainly be better than jail.

Sure enough, there was room for Rosita at the Puerto Rico facility, but to my indignant horror, I was advised that no one could spare the $75 for the plane ticket she would need to reach it. The money just wasn't available.

Meanwhile Rosita was getting jumpy, the way a junkie does who needs a fix.

"Look," I reassured her, speaking more from faith than from reason, "don't worry. We're going to get you to Puerto Rico. We'll pray about it, and we'll get the money."

Rosita stared at me uncertainly. She wanted to be helped, but I could tell that she also wanted drugs, and she was beginning to doubt my glib promises.

"It's going to be all right," I said firmly. "Come on!" And with that, I dragged her to a subway entrance where I took my stand and began asking strangers for money.

"Please," I'd beg of a scurrying commuter, "give something to save this girl's life."

But I honestly thought a few of the people I accosted were going to call the police. They were certain I was either running a confidence game or was insane.

Others shouldered me away with disgust.

"A couple of addicts," they convinced themselves, "trying to raise money for drugs."

But out of each dozen or so people who passed, one or two would donate something, sometimes nickels and dimes, sometimes dollars, until at last I had the price of Rosita's ticket and could put her on a plane for Puerto Rico.

After the plane had gone, it did cross my mind that she might never report to the center. Had I humiliated myself by begging for no good reason?

The ugly idea was fleeting as I thought of Ruth Cowgill's act of love and faith the night she'd given me her own bed. No matter what happened, I was confident I'd done the right thing.

Yet, I wasn't so sure that Demi would agree. he might not be pleased at all to learn that his wife had spent her afternoon as a beggar.

But that night when I told him the story, he tenderly approved of what I'd done.

"Honey," he encouraged me, "I'm proud of you. I'm not sure I could have done what you did for that girl. But I know that the Lord was leading you. Otherwise, you never would have gotten the money."

He was thoughtfully quiet for a moment, and then we went on: "Cookie, I know what helping these girls means to you. And I know what saving these girls means to Jesus. So I think maybe we'd better pray together about our next step.

"I think Jesus wants us to do something more for His sake and something more for these girls."

CHAPTER 29

Stepping Out by Faith

At last Demi and I were in total agreement as to the need to do more for women addicts or women who were trying to escape addiction. Yet the question remained: What should we do?

We thought that we were already doing as much as we possibly could. And yet it wasn't nearly enough. Not only was there not enough room in the rehabilitation program to take care of all the girls who needed help, but the ones who were accepted were creating sorry statistics.

For the record was showing what male junkies had long suspected, that women were harder cases than men. They were more apt than their brothers in addiction to drop out of the program and go back to the streets. Results of Teen Challenge work with girls was so discouraging that I would have wondered whether it was even worthwhile, were it not for our own history.

"Suppose Ruth Cowgill and Dave and Don Wilkerson and Sharon and all the rest had given up on me?" I'd ask myself. "Suppose on the day I ran away from the Brooklyn center the staff hadn't prayed all evening for my return. Where would I be now?"

I knew exactly where I'd be. Dead. Physically and spiritually.

So, in spite of all the setbacks and frustration, I continued to ask Jesus, "Lord, how can Demi and I do more for these girls who need you so much?"

The answer came one night when a light knock sounded at our door. Beyond the door panel, I could hear sobs.

"Who is it?" I inquired as I turned the knob.

"Oh, Cookie," our visitor cried, "please let me come in!"

And in stumbled a pregnant junkie we'll call Louise whom we'd only recently placed in a rehabilitation center.

Unmarried, with three children and another imminent, along with possessing a giant-sized addiction, she certainly needed help, but we'd thought she was one of the luckier ones who was well on her way to receiving it. For only the week before, she'd been admitted into the rehabilitation program.

"What's the matter, Louise?" I asked as she continued to cry and shake. "Why have you left the center?"

They don't understand me there," she sobbed. "They are good; kind people who talk about a good, kind Jesus, but they don't understand what I've been through at all. . . They can help the guys, but they just can't imagine what my past has been like, or what it's done to me.

"You understand, because you've been there. The Jesus those other people believe in seems foreign to me, but the Jesus who saved you can save me too.

"Please let me stay here with you. I'll clean your house. I'll do anything."

Demi, who'd been listening non-committally, nodded, and at his nod, I got out sheets and blankets and made a bed for Louise on our sofa. There was no other space for her in our small apartment.

What were we going to do with her? I wasn't sure, but an idea was beginning to form. The Lord was giving me a leading.

I remembered how different I'd felt from the people who first helped me, how hard it had been for me to accept Sharon's counseling, since we'd come from different worlds. If someone who'd come from the streets had been my earliest Christian teacher, perhaps I would have learned more quickly.

Perhaps, I was thinking, the Lord had saved me, had baptized me with the Holy Spirit, had given me my wonderful Demi so that I could use my sordid past to help rehabilitate other girls.

I discussed my idea with Demi who told me that he, too, felt we were being called to minister almost exclusively to girls.

Naturally we told Dave how we felt and, as always, he agreed that if the Lord were leading us, we'd better move along in the direction He'd indicated.

Demi and I were so excited that we began to tell everyone about our hopes. Word of our proposed ministry spread until, marvelously, two offers of help reached us.

The first came from Nicky Cruz who was starting a new ministry in North Carolina for both boys and girls. He asked us to work with him, and the thought was appealing, for Nicky was an old friend.

Yet we hesitated, feeling that we should minister to girls only and that North Carolina was too far removed from the New York streets where girls who most needed help abounded.

Finally, a church from Pennsylvania contacted us with the offer of a farm we could use as a rehabilitation center if it suited our purposes. This offer was irresistible, so Demi and I set out to go to Pennsylvania and look over the fifty-five acre spread we'd been promised.

We found the farm ideal, and we left it feeling elated!

Nevertheless, we did consult Nicky before making a final decision.

Demi and I decided we wanted the farm but, meanwhile, the Lord decided we shouldn't have it. For, after we'd resigned our positions at Teen Challenge, we got word that the farm wasn't available after all. There'd been confusion about the title, and it turned out that those who'd promised it didn't own it at all.

Naturally we were frightfully disappointed, wondering whether this meant that God wanted us to go to North Carolina or perhaps to stay with Teen Challenge.

However, in the midst of our bewilderment, we got a call from Pauline Bernstein, a splendid Christian lady we'd met in Pennsylvania, saying that she knew of a ten-acre farm which was for sale and which, she thought, we ought to see.

Once again, Demi and I hurried off to Pennsylvania, only to discover that there were no buildings on this farm.

Meanwhile, we were working and praying with Louise, who was still a doubtful case. She wanted to be clean; she wanted to give up drugs and her life on the streets. Yet she was still drawn to her old ways, drawn so strongly that we were often afraid the streets would finally claim her. If only we could get her out of New York, out to the country... how much easier her rehabilitation would be!

Demi and I were still in Pennsylvania after visiting the ten-acre farm when the Holy Spirit took action which set our course. I was sitting in our motel room, idly thumbing through a newspaper and wondering whether we'd actually been led to minister exclusively to girls or whether we'd misinterpreted the inspiration we'd gotten from God, when the name of a church caught my attention. It literally jumped out at me: The Taxville Full Gospel Church.

"Demi," I said, "I know what we are supposed to do. We're supposed to ask the Taxville Full Gospel Church for help."

"The what??" he responded.

"The Taxville Full Gospel Church," I repeated. "I just know its people are going to help us."

Demi knew me too well to wonder how I knew that these people were going to be our earthly angels. He knew that I felt the Holy Spirit was telling me something.

So he telephoned the Rev. Elwood Bell, pastor of the Taxville church, and asked if we could talk with him.

We certainly could!! In fact, the Rev. Bell and his spirit-filled congregation became so enthusiastic about our plans for a rehabilitation project for girls that they actually seemed grateful that we were offering them a chance to participate.

During a meeting with Mr. and Mrs. Bell and Pauline Bernstein in the Bell's living room, we chose a name for our ministry, "New Life for Girls," and formed at least the skeleton of a board of directors.

Next, of course, we had to find a place in which girls could be given new lives, and nothing suitable was yet in sight. Demi and I were spending much of our time on the roads between New York and York,

Pennsylvania, usually with Louise on the back seat, because we didn't want to leave her alone.

Meanwhile, Pauline was inspecting every parcel of land for sale in the York area. And one day she called, obviously excited.

"This time I know we've found the right place," she declared. "It's a twenty-seven acre place near York with two small houses, a barn, a toolshed, and a swimming pool. It's been a gentleman's country retreat. It's. . . "

Without allowing Pauline the time also to tell me that the farm cost $40,000, considerably more than the $150 which made up our life savings, I interrupted. "We'll be down. Right away!"

So down we went, one more time, determined to acquire the home for addicted girls which we felt so strongly the Lord had promised us. Blind faith assured us He wanted us to have it, that we needed it for His work, and so He would give it to us.

However, in Pennsylvania, we found that it took more than blind faith (as a matter of fact, $10,000) to acquire the farm. The $10,000 would only be a down payment, of course, and another $30,000 would be due before we'd have a clear title to the property.

We could see absolutely no hope of raising such astronomical sums; yet, still acting on faith, we turned over our $150 as a binder.

CHAPTER 30

New Life For Girls

Spiritually, we claimed the little farm for the Lord, but literally claiming it was another matter. For our small savings were barely enough to place a binder on

on it which wouldn't hold it long. The owner wanted $40,000 for property, with twenty-five percent down and, to us, $10,000 seemed as unobtainable as a million.

Nevertheless, we turned over the binder fee and continued to claim the farm in Jesus' name.

Meanwhile we talked to everybody—mostly to God—about our hope of establishing a rehabilitation center for women junkies who so desperately needed help. And, by degrees, donations began to trickle in from New York where friends were spreading our story, from the Midwest where more friends were doing likewise, and from members of the Taxville church and their friends.

While the money seeped and then poured in, Demi, our children, Louise and another girl, moved into a house we'd rented on the farm. And within two months after we'd settled there, we had the $10,000 for the down payment!

We walked into the bank thrilled and excited, certain that the $10,000 was a sure sign that God was going to bless our specialized ministry. However, when we put down our money, the bank refused to take it. Because of our backgrounds and the fact that we had no jobs, Demi and I were considered such poor credit risks that couldn't get the mortgage for the remaining $30,000.

With our $10,000, we'd thought that the farm would be ours—God's—but ours to use. But now we were being told that the bank wouldn't carry our note.

Returning to our rented home, we had to face the fact that there was no earthly way for us to buy the farm we needed so badly. Yet we knew there was still a heavenly way, for all things are possible with God. So we continued to pray, not only for money but for faith to keep our dream alive while we waited for the money to come in.

God answered for, before our binder expired, two friends in New York loaned us $10,000 each and, with a $30,000 down payment, the bank agreed to finance the remaining $10,000 of the purchase price.

Crowded to the utmost, we'd thought we could only accomodate twelve girls, but soon we were caring for seventeen, and finally for twenty-six!

We enclosed the carport to give us more space. Then we made another modest addition to our cottage but still we kept running out of room, for there were always more girls needing help than there was available shelter.

Yet we couldn't bear to turn a girl away.

At first, we operated somewhat on a trial and error basis. For example, because I'd hated the work details when I first went into the Teen Challenge program, I was reluctant to assign chores to the girls on our farm. But we soon found out that they were happier and less restless when they were kept busy. So we, too, set up a schedule of work that had to be done.

In our new ministry, Demi and I had to learn through on-the-job training; however, we knew one thing from the start. Any girl coming into New Life For Girls had to come off drugs cold turkey. Prayer, not methadone, would be the only substitute for dope on our farm. And alcohol and tobacco were as forbidden as heroin on our premises.

Volunteer workers pitched in to help us while the community extended an astonishing love and generosity.

Most people in our area had probably never seen a Puerto Rican until we came, and yet, almost without exception, they warmly welcomed these very strange strangers in their midst. Whether white, black, or shades in between, they gave us moral and material support.

Once, when we were completely out of food and money, a neighbor appeared with groceries, bringing not just the essentials but special treats such as he would buy for his own family. He even brought orange juice—something I hadn't tasted in weeks.

He'd gotten a message from the Lord, "When you get your paycheck, take food to New Life For Girls," so that's what he'd done.

There were times when we thought we couldn't make our mortgage payments but always, at the last minute, God saved us and our ministry. Just in time, using the generosity of our friends, He'd meet our material needs.

Meanwhile, however, we were being tested with emotional burdens which were worse than our financial problems. We discovered that some of the very people who'd known us longest and best (or so we thought), acquaintances whom we'd judged to be good Christians, were spreading the word that we were a front for a drug distributor.

Our benefactor, Pauline Bernstein, owned a factory, and according to the malicious rumor, the factory was making dope which Demi and I were dispensing!

Part of the ugly rumor stemmed from an honest mistake because, through unfortunate coincidence, someone with a name similar to hers was involved in a drug operation. But, I'm sorry to say, part of the rumor arose out of jealousy.

Some acquaintences whom we'd thought to be our supporters were actually jealous of our increasing success, so they were willing to believe and to repeat the worst about us.

The authorities took no notice of these charges, but I was so hurt that I became physically ill, even to the point of requiring hospitalization.

Though the county and state never suspected us of violating anti-drug laws, we were suspected of violating the state health code, and as a result we were almost closed down.

We realized that we were terribly crowded in our cottage and yet we couldn't bear to turn away a girl who needed shelter and prayer. So finally thirty girls, plus my family, were packed into a house designed for about three people.

We used the living room as a chapel. Ten girls were sleeping on the floor. But we were enduring the conditions happily, because the Lord had already shown Demi that soon we should build a new building and that He'd give us the means to do it.

After my salvation, I'd seen countless evidences of how God could change lives, beginning with evidence of my own life which was turned so completely upside down that the New York policeman I'd slashed became my friend and used to set up chairs for us when we held street rallies in the ghettos.

The dealer I'd helped mug, who promised to kill me, prayed with me when we met again at Teen Challenge; while the junkie who'd threatened to throw me off the top of a building was converted to Christ and asked me as well as God to forgive him.

So, even before we began our ministry I knew how God could heal tortured sinners. As a matter of fact, it was only because of this knowledge that Demi and I set up our ministry.

But, as I began to see how wonderfully the Lord was transforming the addicts who came to us, my knowledge of His goodness increased, and so did my determination to reach out even further in more effective ways, if God willed it.

After telling Demi that we should build a new building large enough for our needs, the Lord made construction possible.

Some of the girls that came to us were sent by clergymen, some by courts, some by parents, some by their own sense of self-preservation and some by their own desire to become new creatures through Christ.

Lisa was a big, mean black girl from a big, mean family. She came to us from a criminal clan, notorious not only in its neighborhood, but throughout the city for its ruthlessness and often cruel disregard of law.

Lisa, herself a heroin user, was a killer who'd done time for a murder so vicious that it had been featured in a crime magazine. Her reputation was so fearsome that, when she walked down a street, its toughest habitues got out of her way. And still she managed to get into fights!

Finally, after a stint in jail, she was referred to New Life For Girls were she accepted Christ and was freed from her addiction.

The conversion and transformation of Lisa was a miracle made possible only through God's love, and a number of people recognizing it as such were brought to Jesus through her example.

Just as I'd become a new creature, Lisa became one too—no longer bitter and vicious, she became so prayerful and loving that everyone who'd known her in her pre-Christian days was amazed.

The backgrounds of the girls who came to us were very diverse, for drug addiction isn't confined to any particular race, economic strata or educational level. One of the women who came to us was a nurse who, while working at a drug treatment facility where methadone was dispensed, experimented with it and became hooked.

As I've mentioned, I'm determinedly against the use of methadone in the treatment of addicts, because it's nothing more than a cheaper fix.

Another drug victim who's been helped to a new life was a policewoman assigned to the narcotics squad. After a drug bust, she gave way to curiosity and sampled the evidence which became the beginning of her addiction.

Another, still in her mid-teens, was a runaway who'd been shuttled by a criminal conspiracy to New York to work as a prostitute until she became pregnant by one of her clients. She didn't know which one.

Some of the girls who came to us had fallen in love, been seduced and deserted, and to ease their heartbreak had turned to drugs.

Some girls began their addiction with valium given

to them by reputable doctors to relieve bad cases of "nerves."

There's a limitless number of paths to addiction—but only one sure path to release—Jesus.

Cissy came from a Mexican American family and was raped when she was only five years old. Hardly understanding what had happened, she never told her mother. But the experience became a phychological wound which festered and, to a degree, poisoned her life. She was raped again at age eleven and, as result of that incident, was so disturbed that, when a soldier offered her opium when she was fourteen, she accepted it without reservation.

From opium she went on to other drugs, developing a habit which she eventually supported as part of a three-member gang. The trio stole cars in Arizona, traded them in Mexico for heroin and, after taking care of their own needs, sold the remainder of the drug in the United States.

Let Cissy tell you what happened to her in her own words:

"We made it a point never to stop in Mexico with the heroin," she says. "We'd always put the stuff in the gas tank and cross the border before we'd get out of the van.

"But one night we were really sick, needing fixes so badly, that we pulled off the road while we were still in Mexico. We got into the back of the camper—me and a Mexican guy named Pancho and a black fellow named Virgil—and started cooking up our heroin.

"That's what we were doing when the back door flew open, and there was a big, fat Mexican with a Thompson machine gun pointed at us. He looked like he wanted to kill us right away, but instead he dragged us out and took us in to the jail in Nogales.

"They told us there that they'd let us go for $2,000. So we gave $2,000 to a Mexican lawyer, but that didn't do any good. After we'd been beaten a couple of times, they took everything we had and locked us in the prison at Hermisillo.

"I was there about ten months. It was an earthly hell. You could get heroin or anything else in the prison.

"If someone would pay $20, he could take a prisoner into one of the conjugal visiting rooms and do anything he wanted to do. The rooms were only about five by fourteen feet and covered with blood. You might be beaten or molested sexually or anything in one of those little rooms. Anything for the price of $20.

"Once while I was down there, a major riot broke out in the prison. I ran and got as far as the fence but, by that time, the Mexican army had arrived and was shooting.

"As I reached the top of the fence, I was shot in the side. I ran into a dormitory and into a bathroom, but I was hit again by a ricocheting bullet. Soldiers were shooting like crazy. Bullets were flying everywhere.

"Then, for about five days after the riot, guards were beating and torturing everybody who might have been responsible. I think I would have died in that prison if my brothers hadn't smuggled me out.

"There was a workshop in the prison to which people could bring their cars to be reupholstered and so forth, so my brothers had a secret compartment built into an automobile which they brought down. They got me into the compartment and drove back across the border. It was that simple."

Later Cissy spent thirteen months in the Arizona State Prison, but she remembers it as almost heavenly when compared with the Mexican penitentiary.

She was sentenced to prison in Arizona for grand theft after she broke into a drug store. At that time, she was not yet twenty-one!

Though her life had been short up to that point, she badly needed a new one.

Cissy was in a mental hospital when a preacher told her about me. Now she's completed our program and is a fine, beautiful, Christian wife and mother.

Another of our girls we'll call Melba was married to a black revolutionary who was killed. To help her through her heartbreak, she turned to drugs, including heroin and acid. She became so messed up that she killed her own child. Or, at least, she was convicted of the killing, though she says she can't remember it at all.

Before her sentencing, she went into a catatonic state. She neither saw nor heard nor reacted to anything. She was like the living dead. Sent to a hospital for the criminally insane, she was subjected to ally kinds of therapy including shock treatment. But for four years she remained in a trance-like condition.

Neither her mother nor her surviving child could get any sort of response from her.

Meanwhile some official papers connected with her case crossed the desk of a man in Albany, New York, who was filled with the Holy Spirit. He remembered having read about Melba in the New York City papers at the time of her arrest, and he felt a strong impulse to go minister to her.

He knew the ugly details of the crime of which she was convicted. He knew that she was catatonic. Yet the Lord seemed to be telling him to go to the hospital and read the Bible to this mentally, emotionally and spiritually dead girl.

The trip between his office and hospital took two

hours each way, yet every day for six months he traveled to Melba's bedside and read Scriptures to her. Month after month, he got no reaction but, at last, after half a year of repeated effort, he saw tears rolling down her cheeks.

"You can hear me?" he asked. He thought that she nodded, "yes."

"Melba," he said, "Jesus loves you; He loves you very much."

The man didn't know how much she understood of what he was saying, but he continued to pray for her and to talk to her. And by the next day she was definitely showing signs of improvement, coming out of her trance.

Finally, four and a half years after her conviction, the state decided she was well enough to be sentenced.

Before the date set for sentencing, Melba's attorney asked the judge to consider sending her to New Life For Girls for at least a year before he sent her to prison. The judge, however, would not consider it.

Christians who'd heard Melba's story were praying for her and, just before she was to be sentenced, God acted in her behalf.

The judge who was so determined that she go straight to prison, was transferred, while the district attorney (who was equally unsympathetic) suffered a death in his family which forced him to turn her case over to someone else.

Thus, when Melba appeared for sentencing, she faced a new prosecutor and a new judge who was willing to send her to New Life For Girls for one year, while the court investigated her case further.

A year later she went back before the judge who'd been getting dozens of letters testifying to the change in Melba's character.

When she came before the bench, the judge asked if she had anything to say, and she definitely did.

"Your honor," she told him, "I've been a drug addict, a prostitute and, I suppose, a murderer. But I want you and everyone who hears about this case to know that the Melba who was all those things no longer exists.

"I'm a new creature in Christ, because Jesus has changed my life."

Well, the judge gave her five years probation in custody of New Life For Girls. She finished her probation period several years ago, and today she is a wonderful mother and wife.

EPILOGUE

Every day is busy, rich with activity and work. It is very satisfying. But in the midst of enjoying the work of God, I have learned to recognize a subtle temptation. It is all too easy to get wrapped up in working for God, but not with God.

The Holy Spirit has used that insight to reshape my direction and ministry.

This reshaping began a few years ago. I began to see that our ministry in Pennsylvania was finished. But, at the time, I didn't recognize it and wouldn't give it up.

Well, anyone who has walked with the Lord for any number of years knows, He has a way of shifting our viewpoint to His. His concern is that we do His perfect will. As I look back on it, even with my stubbornness, God was beginning to adjust my perspective.

He combined many factors to finally get through to me. Circumstances began to pile up. My health started to decline. There were problems in the family. The financial support of the ministry wasn't what it needed to be. My husband was complaining, with good reason, that he was losing me to my ministry.

I felt like Job. So-called friends had deserted me. I was physically and emotionally drained. I was on the road raising funds more than I was home. Neglect of many important aspects of my life and family were beginning to emerge. We were still living on the grounds of New Life for Girls, so I virtually had no time off, no privacy, and no family life with my husband and children.

Finally, the Lord was getting through to me. I began to see that my priorities were wrong. For others the solution might have been different. For us leaving New Life for Girls was the best alternative.

I'm so grateful that after we learn the lesson God wants to teach us at a given time in our lives, He directs us from there. He led us to Dallas and to Chaplain Ray, who put my first book in every prison in the United States. He and his wife Leola were to us what Ananias must have been to Paul in Damascus--a soothing source of comfort, help, and insight.

In addition God used a James Robison crusade

to completely release from strongholds of sickness, discouragement, and depression in which I had been held for almost three years and a half.

I have entered a new phase of my ministry that combines, in a fresh way, everything God has done in my ministry in the past. We have incorporated under the title of Cookie Rodriguez New Life Ministries.

The arena of the minstry will be prisons, churches, and the streets. I will hold meetings in men's prisons, but our primary emphasis will be to women's institutions. In addition to evangelistic services, I will hold seminars for Christian sisters in prison, covering such topics as bitterness, loneliness, homosexuality, restoring self-image, and living the Christian life in prison.

Church people are also hurting. With the experiences I have had in the last few years, I am looking forward to sharing with fellow believers the insights that God has taught me.

Now, with my priorities right, I will limit traveling to a few days each month.

Demi is my earthly strength and comfort. His parents and his sister and brother-in-law have moved to Dallas to help us in the ministry. My children have been such a joy, especially since I have learned to appreciate motherhood.

Dondi has become a special blessing to me. He made our whole family happy several years ago when he married a wonderful girl who has become like a daughter to Demi and me. Dondi has grown from a sickly, illness-scarred infant to a handsome, healthy young man. The Lord has also given him tremendous talent for music. In fact he and a musical group he is forming are planning to accompany me on ministry trips as often as possible.

Of course, we still have our other three children at home: Danny, 16; Crissy, 14; and Genie, 12. In addition, the Lord gave us Anita when, at the age of nine, her mother left her with us. She is now 20 and married. My grandmother is now 85 and continually serving the Lord.

What a wonderful life we have! Everytime I look at my husband and children, I realize they are God's greatest blessings to me. The Lord is so good! He has given His new life to so many. I'm grateful I am among them. He is not finished with me yet, so this is not the last chapter, because God is still working in my life.

Cookie and Demi surrounded by their family (from left): Crissy, Anita, Melanie, Dondi, Danny, and Genie.

Chaplain Ray
International Prison Ministry
P.O. Box 63
Dallas, TX 75221